TOP DAWGS
UW-STEVENS POINT'S 2004-2005 NATIONAL CHAMPIONSHIP SEASON

Stevens Point Journal

KCI SPORTS VENTURES, LLC
SAVOY, IL

PRODUCTION CREDITS

Front cover: UW-Stevens Point head coach Jack Bennett and the six seniors celebrate their second national championship. Photos courtesy of Tom Charlesworth.

Copyright 2005 KCI Sports Ventures, LLC

All rights reserved. No part of this publication may be reproduced or transmitted in any form or by any means, electronic or mechanic, including photocopying, recording, or any information storage and retrieval system, without written permission from KCI Sports Ventures, LLC.

ISBN: 0-9758769-3-7

Published By:
KCI Sports Ventures, LLC
1402 Quail Run Drive
Savoy, IL 61874

Editor: Peter J. Clark
Photo Editor: Bret Kroencke
Cover Design: Terry Neutz Hayden
Book Layout and Design: Terry Neutz Hayden
Editing/Proofing: Tim Sullivan

Photos Courtesy of Stevens Point Journal unless otherwise noted. Photos for Final Four courtesy of Tom Charlesworth and Ryan Coleman/D3Hoops.com. Photos of Marquette game courtesy of UWSP Sports Information Office. Photos for Eau Claire game courtesy of Rick Mickelson. Photos of Stout game courtesy of Layne Pitt and the UW-Stout Sports Information Office. Photos of Platteville game courtesy of Any McNeil and the UW-Platteville Sports Information Office.

We have made every effort to provide appropriate credit for all photographs herein. However, in the event of any inadvertent omission of credit, we will be pleased to make the necessary corrections in future printings.

Printed and bound by Worzalla Publishing, Stevens Point, WI.

Andrew Dowd   Harold Goodridge   Helen Jungwirth   Tom Kujawski   Kelly McBride   Lisa Nellessen-Lara

A Special Thanks to the *Stevens Point Journal* Staff

University of Wisconsin-Stevens Point athletics are a key part of the Stevens Point Journal's sports pages. But few stories captured the heart of the community as strongly as the Pointer men's basketball team's dream journey, which culminated in *back-to-back* NCAA Division III championships in 2004 and 2005. Already a community favorite, the team's rise to the top fascinated sports fans of all ages. Throughout the season, Pointer mania enveloped the city. The mad rush for tickets was unlike anything the university had ever seen. Fans camped out at the ticket counter to be first in line and "Got an extra ticket?" became the most repeated phrase in Stevens Point. Journal staff were equally enthralled, and proud to play a role in bringing Pointer coverage to its readers. At the grocery store, church gatherings, classrooms and around the dining room table – the Pointers were the dominant conversation, and readers wanted more. The Journal responded. Coverage of the team began on the sports pages at the beginning of the season, but quickly spilled over onto the front page. We tried to cover all the angles – where to get the best seats, how to spot the die-hard fans, and the parents, wives and assistants behind the team and Coach Jack Bennett. Sports and news staff, circulation, creative and advertising departments combined their efforts to put out a special cheer card commemorating the team's success, our gift to fans during the Sweet 16 game. It truly was a team effort.

The Pointers will be back in 2006 — there'll be some new faces on the court along with a few favorites. We'll be back as well, to bring the Pointer coverage readers demand. What a ride.

Lisa Nellessen-Lara
Managing Editor

Al Shane   Jill Steinke   Nathan Vine   Scott Williams   Doug Wojcik

ACKNOWLEDGEMENT

The publisher would like to offer a "very special thank you" to the following for their efforts and contributions to this book:

Head Coach Jack Bennett, his staff and all of the UWSP players—without your outstanding efforts there wouldn't be a book. Frank O'Brien and the UWSP athletic department for their assistance and support of this book. Special thanks to Jim Strick who continues to work in relative anonymity as one of the finest Sports Information Directors in the country. The staff at the *Stevens Point Journal,* led by the tireless Helen Jungwirth, who have rededicated themselves to outstanding coverage of all Pointer sports. Scott Williams, Nathan Vine and all of the other talented writers for recapturing an unforgettable season. Doug Wojcik, Tom Kujawski, Tom Charlesworth and all of the other talented photographers who contributed photos to this project. Terry Neutz-Hayden for yet another great design job. Bret and Kate Kroencke for keeping things running smoothly in Savoy. Kim Deuel and the staff at Worzalla Publishing who continue to be a pleasure to work with.

Thanks to Corey Konkol, Tim Voorheis, Shoe Sullivan . . . Wade Rewey, Scott Bucholtz and Rory Menzer . . . Pat Leahy, Mike Laudon, Harry Gleason and all the others I may be overlooking, but whose efforts are certainly much appreciated.

Peter Clark
Publisher

TOM CHARLESWORTH

TOP DAWGS
CONTENT

ACKNOWLEDGEMENTS	4
FOREWORD by Dick Bennett	6
INTRODUCTION by Terry Porter	7

PRESEASON	**10**
MARQUETTE EXHIBITION	**12**
THE SEASON	
Midway Classic	
UWSP 65, Southwestern (TX) 42	17
UWSP 70, University of Chicago 58	18
UWSP 70, Lakeland College 59	19
UWSP 75, Ripon College 53	20
Kyle Grusczynski Feature	**21**
Wisconsin Intercollegiate Athletic Conference	
UWSP 55, UW-Platteville 44	23
UWSP 71, UW-Eau Claire 50	25
UWSP 65, UW-River Falls 50	27
UWSP 75, UW-Stout 52	28
Sentry Classic	
UWSP 86, Viterbo University 54	30
UWSP 82, Wisconsin Lutheran 42	32
Eric Maus Feature	**33**
UWSP 63, UW-Whitewater 71	35
UWSP 82, Marian College 57	36
UWSP 65, UW-La Crosse 49	37
Pointers Reach out to Fans	38
UWSP 77, UW-Superior 42	39
Tamaris Relerford Feature	**40**

UWSP 69, UW-Oshkosh 44	42
UWSP 79, Edgewood College 49	44
UWSP 63, UW-La Crosse 62 OT	45
Nick Bennett Feature	**46**
UWSP 58, UW-Platteville 72	48
UWSP 64, UW-Stout 52	49
UWSP 83, UW-Eau Claire 55	50
Jason Kalsow Feature	**51**
UWSP 75, UW-Whitewater 64	53
Free Throw Brings End to Record	55
UWSP 83, UW-Superior 58	56
UWSP 94, UW-River Falls 66	57
Pointers Meet Younger Fans	59
UWSP 59, UW-Oshkosh 74	60
WIAC Tournament	
UWSP 88, UW-Superior 68	61
UWSP 65, UW-Oshkosh 59	63
UWSP 87, UW-Whitewater 77	65
NCAA Division III Tournament	
Preview	67
Pointer Mania	68
UWSP 79, Lawrence University 45	70
Pointers to Host NCAA Sectional	74
Point a Great Tourney Site	75

Pointers' Offense Fights On	76
Tickets Go Quickly	77
For the Love of the Team	78
Pointers Work on Mind Game	79
UWSP Assistants Feature	**80**
NCAA Division III Sectionals	
UWSP 81, University of Puget Sound (WA) 63	82
UWSP 61, Trinity (TX) 55	86
Pointers Lead Lands On Rookie Hicklin	92
NCAA Division III Final Four Semifinals	
Preview	93
Pointers Receive Warm Welcome	95
Die-Hard Fans Don't Miss The Bus	96
UWSP 81, York (PA) 58	98
NCAA Division III National Championship Game	
UWSP 73, Rochester (NY) 49	101
Krull Comes Up Big	113
UWSP Fans Welcome Champs Home	114
AWARDS	**116**
The Epitome of a Complete Team	117
Season Stats	118
Ode to the Pointers	119

DOUG WOJCIK

FOREWORD

Dick Bennett

Winning a basketball championship at any level is a difficult thing to do. You must have an experienced coach, players who are mentally tough and willing to pay the price to be successful, and a dose of good luck to stay healthy throughout the season.

Attaining back-to-back national championships coming out of a league as difficult as the Wisconsin Intercollegiate Athletic Conference, going unbeaten throughout the playoffs while taking your opponent's best shot each night, and dominating at the Final Four with a record-setting margin of victory is unheard of. Yet that is exactly what the 2004-05 UWSP men's basketball team achieved.

This ball club was a **team** in the truest sense of the word. Eddie Fogler, the former South Carolina head coach, mentioned during the championship broadcast that UWSP was one of the best passing teams he had ever seen—at any level. He was right. The ability to find the open man on offense without any regard for who scores the points, underscores a theme of selflessness at Stevens Point that is so very difficult to accomplish yet so vital to a team's overall success.

Hardworking, determined, and humble are only a few characteristics that describe some of the better teams I've been fortunate enough to coach. The 2004-05 Pointer team certainly embodies those same characteristics. Possessing a blend of senior leaders and supporting underclassmen, this team always seemed to stay the course when the waters ran rough around them. Not missing a beat when they lost a starting point guard during the NCAA tournament speaks to that point.

I couldn't be prouder of or happier for my brother, Jack. He has set a standard of excellence at UWSP every coach in the game aspires to but few reach. I am sure Jack would agree that the journey was made even more memorable because he was able to share it with his youngest son, Nick, whose talents would make any coach very happy. The awards and accolades that will be bestowed on the players and coaches are all well-deserved.

I know that the great Stevens Point fans realize how special this group of young men is and appreciate their sacrifice and efforts in lifting UWSP basketball to such impressive heights. Jack and his team have definitely established the benchmark for Stevens Point basketball for years to come.

Dick Bennett
Head Coach, Washington State University
Head Coach, UWSP 1976-1985

DOUG WOJCIK   TOM CHARLESWORTH   TOM CHARLESWORTH

INTRODUCTION

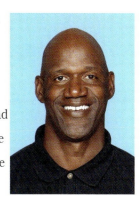

It was with great pride that I followed Coach Jack Bennett's team last year as they made their incredible run to the school's first NCAA Men's Basketball National Championship. Fond memories of playing in the national tournament in Kansas City and the many great friendships forged during my playing career at UWSP came rushing back.

Having been fortunate enough to watch the Pointers play their preseason exhibition game against Marquette at the Bradley Center, I had a feeling the 2004-05 team was special. Not only was the physical talent of the UWSP players readily apparent, but more importantly, the intangibles were in place-unselfishness, toughness, and a willingness to accept nothing less than the maximum effort every time down the court. All are key ingredients in making a run to repeat as NCAA champs.

Terry Porter

When you have success, expectations skyrocket, yet this Pointer team found a way to deliver. I congratulate Coach Bennett, his staff and the Pointer players for their outstanding season and impressive Final Four performance. Their focus and will to win in the second half of the championship game were nothing short of amazing.

This book is a fitting tribute to the coaches and players whose accomplishments over the past two years have made a university and community proud.

I hope you enjoy looking back on a very special season.

Terry Porter
Head Coach, Milwaukee Bucks
1985 UWSP Graduate
UWSP Hall of Fame

The publisher would like to offer a special thanks to the following for their continued support of University of Wisconsin Stevens Point Athletics.

DigiCopy
Sentry Insurance
WAOW Channel 9
Point Sports Medicine
Worzalla Publishing
Courtesy Motors

County Market
WSPT/1010 AM
Fairfield Inn
M&I Bank
UWSP Foundation
Anderson, O'Brien, Bertz, Skrenes & Golla
UWSP Alumni Affairs
Don & Tina Peters
Premium Brands, Inc.
US Bank
Sonstra Apartments
UWSP's Men's Basketball Backcourt Club
Commercial Roofing

POINTERS

2004-2005 NATIONAL CHAMPS

Thanks for the memories

PHOTOS COURTESY OF RYAN COLEMAN

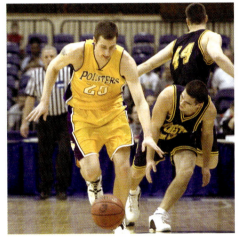

Preseason
TOUGH TO DEFEND
Pointers begin quest for second national title

Top: *Head Coach Jack Bennett puts his team through a defensive drill. The Pointers will try to become only the third school in Division III history to repeat as national champions.*

Below: *Jason Kalsow shoots the game-winning jumper with 0.2 seconds left in the 2004 Division III title game to give UWSP a 84-82 win over Williams College.*

Opposite Page: *Jon Krull lays the ball in during drills.*

By Scott Williams

Jason Kalsow doesn't remember a lot about the shot.

All the forward on the University of Wisconsin-Stevens Point men's basketball team can recall is his team ran a play it had called hundreds of times before.

Immune to all the hysteria around him, Kalsow calmly drained a fade-away jumper with 0.2 seconds left in the Division III title game to give the Pointers a 84-82 win over Williams (Mass.) College.

The shot secured the school's first NCAA Division III national championship in the sport, as bedlam erupted on the court in Salem, Va.

"I didn't remember shooting the ball, but it was nice after it went in," said Kalsow, who returns for his senior season as a candidate for the National Player of the Year.

"Their player played it the way he should. The only shot I had was a turn-around jumper. The worst thing that could have happened was overtime."

On paper, UWSP seems to have all the pieces in place for a serious run at back-to-back national titles. All five starters back from a team that finished 29-5, and set a school record for victories in a season.

But the UWSP coaches and players insist there are no guarantees.

Can the Pointers expect to shoot 56.3 percent from the field during six NCAA tournament games? Is senior guard Nick Bennett going to maintain his torrid scoring pace of 25.5 points during the tournament and 60-percent shooting from 3-point range?

Pointer coach Jack Bennett realizes his team has a tough act to follow.

"What we did takes on more meaning with time. But I feel we built a resume last season to dream about repeating," said Bennett, who owns a 171-53 career record at the school.

"We tell our guys that we set a nice standard last year. As long as we play to our potential and keep getting better, the results will take care of themselves."

The Pointers have the confidence of just about every Division III basketball observers. In nearly any preseason poll, they are sitting at the top. UWSP is the unanimous choice to win the brutal Wisconsin Intercollegiate Athletic Conference in a vote of the league's sports information directors.

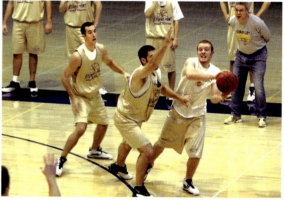
DOUG WOJCIK

PHOTO COURTESY OF UWSP SPORTS INFORMATION OFFICE

That honor went to River Falls last season after a four-year run by the Pointers. It's a title they want back.

"We came up short in the conference and we want to regain that," Kalsow said. "Plus, we just want to get better every game and be ready for tournament time which is the ultimate thing."

Kalsow and Nick Bennett are the building blocks.

A 6-foot-7 senior forward from Huntley, Ill., Kalsow averaged 17.2 points a year ago and needs 402 points this season to become the school's all-time leading scorer.

Nick Bennett, a 6-5 guard/forward, was the Most Valuable Player in the Division III Final Four after pouring in 30 points in the championship game. He also scored at a clip of 17.2 points last season.

Both players were first-team All-WIAC selections last year and named a Street & Smith's preseason All-American.

"I think Jason and Nick will go down as the two best players on the same team not only in this league, but in Pointer history," coach Bennett said. "But what separates them is they truly put the team ahead of everything else."

In many respects, it's the rest of the team that allows Kalsow and Nick Bennett to do their thing.

Eric Maus, a 6-9 senior center, and 6-4 sophomore forward Jon Krull are willing and content to handle the little things that may not show up in the stat sheet but are critical in the win column.

When needed, any of the eight or nine players currently in the rotation can make a difference. Krull, for example, emerged from the shadows with a 25-point effort in the national semifinals.

"I think Jon has a chance to be a scorer. He's one of the most unflappable kids I've been around," said coach Bennett. "Maus is the consummate defensive player. We'd like to see him hunt down his shot a little more."

Rounding out the senior class are point guard Tamaris Relerford (5-8) and jack-of-all-trades Kyle Grusczynski, a 6-5 transfer from the University of Wisconsin.

Relerford and Grusczynski, along with 5-10 freshman Shawn Lee, will share the responsibilities at point guard. Grusczynski also has the versatility to move to the wing or post.

"All we want from our point guards is to get us into our offense and set the tone on defense," Bennett said. "We need consistency and toughness there."

Rarely do teams win championship without depth, and the Pointers are no exception.

Junior Brian Bauer, a 6-5 bruiser from Auburndale, and 6-6 forward Mike Prey are being counted on to give Kalsow and Maus a breather in the post.

Another player who has opened some eyes is burly, yet athletic, 6-5 freshman forward Gbenga Awe, who attended UW-Milwaukee last year but didn't play basketball.

"The project of finding your rotation is always on-going. There are things you discover over the course of the season,"

DOUG WOJCIK

Bennett said. "I felt like we need one more guard and another big man to help us."

The first auditions will be held Saturday and Sunday when the Pointers participate in the Midway Classic in Chicago.

UWSP is scheduled to meet Southwestern (Texas) in an 8 p.m. tip-off. The consolation and championship games are set for Sunday.

The scary part for teams on the Pointers schedule is coach Bennett is convinced his team can be better this season.

"I think there are a number of things we can improve. I think we can create a few more turnovers," he said. "I believe we can be a little better rebounding team.

"Now we can have a better basketball team and it may not show up in our record."

EXHIBITION
Marquette
POINTERS DARE TO DREAM

UWSP men to play Marquette in exhibition

By Scott Williams

University of Wisconsin-Stevens Point men's basketball coach Jack Bennett received an interesting phone call at his office Monday.

Dick Bennett was on the other end of the line informing his brother about a recent dream.

In the dream, the Bennett brothers, along with current Pointer and Jack's son, senior forward Nick Bennett, played and beat Marquette University in a basketball game.

"Nick is going to have to take all the shots," Jack told his brother.

"Neither Dick nor I can shoot a lick," he added.

Jack Bennett would like nothing more than for the dream to come true, but he understands the harsh reality of the situation is the defending NCAA Division III national champion Pointers have their work cut out for them.

"We have two goals," Jack Bennett said. "First off, we want to be competitive with them. We know what we're up against. We want to look and see if we can maybe compete against a quality Division I program.

"No. 2, we want to feel like we're a better team after the game. A game like this should expose the things we need to work on to become a better team. A loss in a game like this is not as dangerous as not stretching your team."

Not lost on Jack Bennett is the tradition-rich history both schools have on the basketball floor.

Marquette earned a Division I national championship in 1977, and also reached the Final Four in 1973 and most recently in 2002.

A year ago, UW-Stevens Point became the most recent in a long line of Wisconsin Intercollegiate Athletic Conference schools to win a national men's basketball title.

"When I started my coaching career two men jumped out at me - Vince Lombardi and Al McGuire. Both men had a tremendous influence on my coaching because they gave their teams a chance to be successful, albeit in different ways," Bennett said. "One (McGuire) was street smart and the other (Lombardi) ruled with an iron fist. I've taken qualities from both men."

Tonight's exhibition was made possible by a recent change in NCAA philosophy regarding Division I preseason games.

In an effort to discourage games with the Athletes in Action and Marathon Oils of the

Top: The Pointers huddle together prior to the Marquette game.

Below: Senior Tamaris Relerford leads the Pointers out onto the Bradley Center floor.

PHOTO COURTESY OF UWSP SPORTS INFORMATION OFFICE

PHOTO COURTESY OF UWSP SPORTS INFORMATION OFFICE

college basketball world, the NCAA opened up the option of playing Division III schools without penalizing either institution.

When Marquette coach Tom Crean contacted Bennett last spring about the idea of playing an exhibition game this fall, the decision was a "no-brainer," as McGuire might say.

Crean got a first-hand glimpse into the Pointers program last season when he was the featured speaker during a basketball clinic held at Quandt Fieldhouse.

"When they called us, we jumped at it," Bennett said. "I've gotten to know Tom a little bit and we've cultivated a friendship I guess you would call it. It's not like we call each other all the time, but we stay in touch."

With all five starters returning from last year's national championship team, Bennett is eager to see what this season hold in store for the Pointers.

Odds are UWSP probably won't see the kind of size, strength and speed the Golden Eagles present the rest of the season. And in senior point guard Travis Diener, Marquette may arguably have one of the premier floor leaders in the country.

"To play an elite team like Marquette is good financially and from a public relations standpoint," Bennett said. "It's an exhibition game, and while the score means something, the big thing is how competitive we play. Do we force tough shots or get pounded on the boards? Those are the things we're going to look at."

The bottom line, according to Bennett, is the game will help prepare the Pointers for their title defense, and serve as a measuring stick for where they are and where they need to be.

Still, a coach can't help but think "what if."

"After ending last season on such a high, it does cross your mind how we would stack up against the Division II national champion or a Division I team," Bennett said. "Now, we've got an opportunity to see instead of talking about it."

Left: The playing of the national anthem.

Right: Head Coach Jack Bennett works the sidelines as the Pointer bench intently watches the game.

PHOTO COURTESY OF UWSP SPORTS INFORMATION OFFICE

PHOTO COURTESY OF UWSP SPORTS INFORMATION OFFICE

EXHIBITION
Marquette
POINTERS HANG TOUGH

UWSP Within Four with 7 Minutes Left

Below: Eric Maus drains a first half shot against Marquette.

> "I've never seen a Division III team that is that sound and that good. Execution wise they're as good as anyone we play."
>
> —Marquette Head Coach Tom Crean

By Scott Williams

MILWAUKEE - Good basketball is good basketball.

It doesn't matter if it's Division I, Division III or Division XX. The University of Wisconsin-Stevens Point men's basketball team made that perfectly clear Tuesday night.

The defending Division III national champions pushed Marquette University to the limit before succumbing 78-65 in an exhibition game at the Bradley Center.

"I hope the one thing we proved is that we're not a great Division III basketball team, but we proved we're a very good college basketball team," said Pointer senior forward Nick Bennett, who poured in a team-high 27 points and left more than a few onlookers impressed.

For Bennett and the Pointers, the exhibition game was about more than earning respect against the Golden Eagles, who are two years removed from a Final Four appearance of their own.

The game was a feather in the cap of the Wisconsin Intercollegiate Athletic Conference specifically, and the caliber of Division III basketball as a whole.

The outcome only served to validate the long-standing belief that the WIAC is among the best basketball conferences in the country, regardless of division.

"I believe we have the ACC of Division III basketball," Pointers coach Jack Bennett said. "No disrespect to Marquette, but I thought we could win the game. We were able to play them to a standstill and made them keep their starters in until the end."

When Bennett drained a 3-pointer with 7 minutes left in the second half to bring the Pointers within 59-55, Marquette understood UWSP meant business.

"We never referred to them as a Division III team. The last time they played, they cut down the nets," Marquette coach Tom Crean said. "When we scheduled this game we fully anticipated this would be a great game. Execution-wise, they were as good as anybody we play.

"I started coaching in Division III at Alma College in Michigan, and I've never seen a Division III team that sound and that good. Every accolade they get they deserve."

In a sign of ultimate respect, Crean moved All-American point guard candidate Travis Diener to cover Bennett over the final six minutes. Bennett never scored again.

PHOTO COURTESY OF UWSP SPORTS INFORMATION OFFICE

Left: Brian Bauer passes the ball to a posting Jason Kalsow.

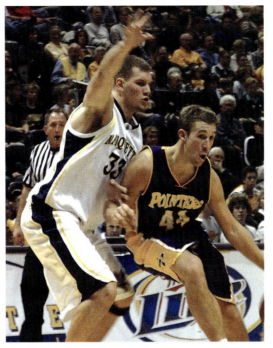

Right: Jason Kalsow drives to the hoop against Chris Grimm in first half action.

Left: Head Coach Jack Bennett and assistant Bob Semling call out instruction on a Pointer inbounds play.

Right: Jon Krull shoots a three-pointer over Marquette's Ryan Amoroso.

Bennett saw the move not so much as a sign of respect, but as sound strategy.

"They were doing everything they could to win the game," Nick Bennett said. "Diener had the quickness and strength to run around and tag me."

Diener was the difference in the game on both ends of the court.

With the senior from Fond du Lac lifting his team on his shoulders, the Golden Eagles outscored UWSP 19-10 over the final seven minutes to finally secure the win.

With a scout from the Houston Rockets on hand, Diener gave him plenty to like with a game-high 32 points and seven assists.

"Travis is everything he is built up to be, and when you see him up close, he is even more," coach Bennett said. "Diener is just darn good. I can see why my brother Dick was sick when he didn't get him at Wisconsin."

Rockets scout Brett Johnson was not only impressed by Diener, but couldn't help but notice Nick Bennett and Jason Kalsow, who chipped in with 23 points and seven rebounds.

"Bennett may be the best non-athletic basketball player I've ever seen," Johnson said. "He can't jump and he's not that quick. But he can think the game as well as anyone."

In the final analysis, the game was what it was - an exhibition.

But the Pointers can come out of the game with their heads held high, and a great starting point to launch their title defense.

"If we had lost by four or squeaked a win out, this isn't our season," Nick Bennett said. "Our season was not about winning an exhibition game against Marquette. We want to improve and try to win a conference championship, and maybe the national title again."

At least one person thinks they have a great chance to repeat.

"They're definitely going to make it back to the Final Four," Johnson said.

GOLDEN EAGLES 78, POINTERS 65

UW-STEVENS POINT (65): Tamaris Relerford 0-3 0-0 0, Nick Bennett 8-18 4-5 27, Jon Krull 3-11 5-6 11, Jason Kalsow 9-18 3-3 23, Eric Maus 2-7 0-0 4, Kyle Grusczynski 0-4 0-0 0, Brian Bauer 0-1 0-0 0, Mike Prey 0-1 0-0 0. Totals 22-63 12-14 65.

MARQUETTE (78): Todd Townsend 2-4 2-2 8, Rob Hanley 0-0 0-1 0, Steve Novak 3-10 0-0 9, Dameon Mason 6-9 1-5 13, Joe Chapman 0-4 0-0 0, Travis Diener 10-16 8-9 32, Marcus Jackson 2-2 0-2 4, Mike Kinsella 1-2 0-0 2, Ousmane Barro 1-3 0-0 2, Ryan Amoroso 3-6 2-2 8. Totals 28-56 13-21 78.

UW-Stevens Point	30	35	- 65
Marquette	43	35	- 78

3-point goals: UWSP 9-26 (Relerford 0-2, Bennett 7-12, Krull 0-3, Kalsow 2-5, Maus 0-1, Grusczynski 0-3), Marquette 9-25 (Townsend 2-4, Novak 3-9, Chapman 0-2, Diener 4-8, Amoroso 0-2). **Total fouls:** UWSP 17, Marquette 19. **Fouled out:** none: **Rebounds:** UWSP 31 (Maus 8), Marquette 42 (Mason 8). **Turnovers:** UWSP 13, Marquette 16.

PHOTO COURTESY OF UWSP SPORTS INFORMATION OFFICE

PHOTO COURTESY OF UWSP SPORTS INFORMATION OFFICE

Top Left: Junior Mike Prey battles for the rebound. UWSP alumnus and Division I official Steve Olson is in the background.

Top Right: Nick Bennett hits one of his seven three-pointers against Marquette.

PHOTO COURTESY OF UWSP SPORTS INFORMATION OFFICE

PHOTO COURTESY OF UWSP SPORTS INFORMATION OFFICE

PHOTO COURTESY OF UWSP SPORTS INFORMATION OFFICE

Bottom Left: Jon Krull ties up a Marquette player to force a jump ball.

Bottom Center: Tamaris Relerford drives past Travis Diener in first half action.

Bottom Right: Former Pointer great and current Milwaukee Bucks head coach Terry Porter caught the action at the Bradley Center versus Marquette.

THE SEASON
MIDWAY CLASSIC

Pointers get easy win in season opener

By Scott Williams

POINTERS 65, SOUTHWESTERN 42

UUW-Stevens Point (1-0)-Relerford, Tamaris 0-2 0-0 0, Bennett, Nick 5-11 1-1 13, Krull, Jon 3-6 0-2 7, Kalsow, Jason 8-10 0-0 17, Maus, Eric 5-8 1-1 11, Lee, Shawn 1-2 0-0 0, Hirsch, Brett 1-5 0-0 2, Kalsow, Brad 2-4 2-2 7, Hicklin, Steve 1-4 0-0 2, Grusczynski, Kyle 0-1 0-0 0, Krautkramer, Cory 1-1 0-0 2, Bouche, Matt 0-2 0-0 0 Bauer, Brian 0-2 0-0 0, Prey, Mike 0-2 0-0 0, Awe, Gbenga 1-2 0-0 2

Southwestern (0-1)-Ty Ragland 1-2 0-0 2, Aaron Bowser 4-10 7-8 15, Danny Franklin 5-10 0-0 12, Dan Slezak 0-2 0-0 0, Robert Cates 1-5 0-0 2, Mike Powell 1-3 1-3 3, Goran Stojcic 1-5 0-0 3, Tony Petronella 0-0 0-0 0, Miles Elsey 0-1 0-0 0, Brandon Daniels 1-3 0-0 2, Tyler Fredericksen 0-1 0-0 0, Hugh Arrington 0-3 0-0 0, Casey Gorder 1-2 1-2 3 Jamonn Little 0-0 0-0 0, Peter Willrich 0-1 0-0 0

UW-Stevens Point	42	23	- 65
Southwestern	15	27	- 42

3-point goals: Southwestern 3-18, Stevens Point 5-21 (Krull 1-2, J. Kalsow 1-3, Relerford 2-2, Bennett 2-6, Grusczynski 0-1, Hicklin 0-3, Lee 0-1, Hirsch 0-1, B. Kalsow 1-2). Total fouls: Southwestern 8, Stevens Point 13. Fouled out: none Rebounds: Southwestern 27 (Cates, Bowser 5), Stevens Point 41 (Maus 7). Turnovers Southwestern 13, Stevens Point 12.

CHICAGO - The University of Wisconsin-Stevens Point men's basketball team took its first step in defending its NCAA Division III national championship with a 65-42 win over Southwestern (Tex.) in the Midway Classic on Saturday.

"It was a terrific way to start the season," UWSP coach Jack Bennett said. "I thought that the fact that we played Marquette in our exhibition well helped in this game tonight."

The Pointers started their season opener by hitting six of their first seven shots and jumped out to a quick 20-2 lead.

UWSP outscored the Pirates 13-0 in the final 5:10 of the first half and grabbed a convincing 42-15 lead at halftime. They then scored the first eight points of the second half to cap off the 21-0 run.

Jason Kalsow led UWSP with 17 points on 8-of-10 shooting from the floor. Nick Bennett added 13 while Eric Maus poured in 11.

"If we can get Maus to score like that more often, I think we'll have the type of balance that we're looking for", Bennett said.

The Pointers found the right touch on the floor as they hit 45.2 percent of their shots, including 17 of 27 in the first half.

UWSP struggled from beyond the arc in the second half, missing all 12 shots from 3-point range, but compensated by hitting 11 of 23 from inside the paint.

On the other end of the court, the Pirates were 31.3 percent from the field, including a dismal 6 for 21 in the opening half.

Aaron Bowser led Southwestern with 15 points. Danny Franklin added 12.

The Pointers are back in action today when they face host University of Chicago.

Bennett said he and Maroons coach Mike McGrath talked about the last time the Pointers and Maroons locked horns - the 2000 NCAA Division III tournament, in which the Pointers won 63-49.

"We talked about that and said that it's not quite the same circumstances as in that game," he said.

"They are big and strong and love to post the guards up. This is the kind of a good test that we want."

THE SEASON
MIDWAY CLASSIC

Kalsow Drains 28 as UWSP Improves to 2-0

By Scott Williams

CHICAGO - Jason Kalsow matched a career-high with 28 points as the University of Wisconsin-Stevens Point men's basketball team improved to 2-0 with a 70-58 victory over the University of Chicago on Sunday to win the Midway Classic championship.

Nick Bennett added 25 points for UWSP, including a 4-for-5 performance from 3-point range.

"They are one of the best duos that have ever put on the purple and gold at UWSP," Pointers coach Jack Bennett said. "They carried the team on their shoulders and there will be nights we have to have them do that."

Chicago had a 38-28 lead with 15:55 left in the second before Kalsow - the tournament's MVP - scored seven straight points to spark a 22-3 Pointer run over the next 8:53. The Pointers hit 17 of 25 shots in the second half and rebounded from a shaky 9 for 28 first half.

"That came because we had a better defense," Bennett said. "Give Chicago credit. They gave us a good challenge and our defense was what picked up our intensity on offense.

Eric Maus led the Pointers with seven rebounds and Kyle Grusczynski chalked up a team-high three assists. Brian Cuttica led the host Maroons with 11 points, including 3 of 9 from 3-point range while Brandon Woodhead added 10.

POINTERS 70, MAROONS 58

UW-Stevens Point (2-0)-Relerford, Tamaris 1-2 0-0 3, Bennett, Nick 8-12 5-6 25, Krull, Jon 4-9 1-1 9, Kalsow, Jason 11-20 6-8 28, Maus, Eric 0-2 0-0 0, Lee, Shawn 0-0 0-0 0, Hirsch, Brett 0-0 0-0 0, Kalsow, Brad 0-2 0-0 0, Hicklin, Steve 0-0 0-0 0, Grusczynski, Kyle 2-4 0-1 5, Krautkramer, Cory 0-0 0-0 0, Bauer, Brian 0-1 0-0 0, Prey, Mike 0-1 0-0 0, Awe, Gbenga 0-0 0-0 0

Chicago (1-1)-Cuttica, Brian 4-11 0-0 11, Woodhead, Brandon 4-9 2-2 10, Waldie, Justin 1-5 3-4 6, Dolezal, Mike 4-6 0-1 8, Vismantas, Jason 0-0 0-0 0, Okonkwo, Uche 0-2 0-0 0, Todd, Jon 0-0 0-0 0, Meyer, Jesse 2-6 0-2 6, Hainje, Nate 2-3 0-0 5, Carmody, Clay 5-9 2-4 12

UW-Stevens Point	42	23	- 65
Chicago	29	29	- 58

3-point goals: Chicago 7-27, Stevens Point 6-11 (Krull 0-1, Relerford 1-2, Bennett 4-5, Grusczynski 1-2, B. Kalsow 0-1). **Total fouls:** Chicago 19, Stevens Point 14. **Fouled out:** none **Rebounds:** Chicago 30 (Waldie 6), Stevens Point 31 (Maus 7). **Turnovers:** Chicago 10, Stevens Point 8.

THE SEASON
NONCONFERENCE

Pointers Down Muskies to Stay Perfect at 3-0

By Scott Williams

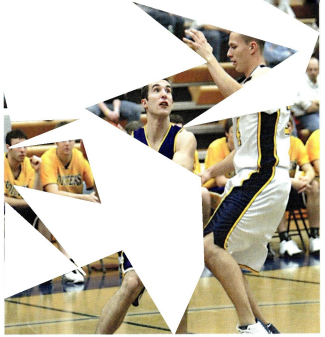

Left: Nick Bennett prepares to go up for a shot over a Lakeland defender.

PHOTO COURTESY OF UWSP SPORTS INFORMATION OFFICE

SHEBOYGAN - The reigning NCAA Division III men's basketball champion University of Wisconsin-Stevens Point remained undefeated with a 70-59 win over Lakeland College on Friday night.

The Pointers improve to 3-0 going into tonight's home opener, where the team will unveil the championship banner against Ripon College.

"It was a good win, but we didn't play particularly crisp," UWSP coach Jack Bennett said. "We found a way to win and that's the mark of a (good) basketball team."

UWSP got 20 points and eight rebounds out of Jason Kalsow and 11 from both Tamaris Relerford and Nick Bennett. Eric Maus contributed 10 points, eight rebounds and six assists for the Pointers.

Nick Zeck scored 19 points for Lakeland (1-2).

UWSP struggled shooting the ball in the first half (36 percent), ending with a 28-23 lead at halftime. Things vastly improved in the second half (53.8 percent), but Lakeland continued to hang around. The Pointers used an 8-2 run with about 2:00 minutes left to close out the ball game.

POINTERS 70, MUSKIES 59

Lakeland (59): Kris Saiberlich 2-8 6-6 11, Danny Ehnert 0-0 0-0 0, Ryan Hiir 2-11 0-0 4, Germaayne James 2-8 0-0 5, Nick Zeck 6-9 7-7 19, Logan Heine 1-1 0-0 2, Nick Howard 3-6 0-0 8, Will Jenson 0-0 0-0 0, Paul Keller 3-5 1-1 7, Craig Zellner 1-3 0-0 3, David Hoerres 0-1 0-0 0. FG: 20-52, 38.5%. FT: 14-14, 100%.

UWSP (70): Tamaris Relerford 3-6 2-2 11, Nick Bennett 2-13 6-7 11, Jon Krull 3-7 2-2 8, Jason Kalsow 7-12 6-8 20, Eric Maus 4-7 2-2 10, Shawn Lee 1-2 0-0 3, Kyle Grusczynski 3-3 0-0 7, Brian Bauer 0-1 0-0 0, Mike Prey 0-0 0-0 0. FG: 23-51, 45.1%. FT: 18-21, 85.7%.

UW-Stevens Point	28	42	- 70
Lakeland	23	36	- 59

3-point goals: Stevens Point 6-14 (Bennett 1-4, J. Kalsow 0-2, Relerford 3-4, Krull 0-1, Lee 1-2, Grusczynski 1-1), Lakeland 5-24. Total fouls: Lakeland 22, Stevens Point 11. Fouled out: none. Rebounds: Lakeland 30, Stevens Point 32 (Maus, J.Kalsow 8). Turnovers: Lakeland 13, Stevens Point 9.

THE SEASON
NONCONFERENCE

Pointers roll at home

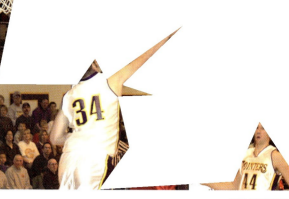

Right: Jon Krull blocks the shot of Ripon guard David McMullen.

TOM KUJAWSKI

By Scott Williams

STEVENS POINT - The University of Wisconsin-Stevens Point men's basketball team unveiled its 2004 national championship banner Saturday night.

More performances like the one the Pointers turned in against Ripon College, and the search will soon be on for more wall space at the Quandt Fieldhouse.

Jason Kalsow scored a team-high 14 points and 13 of the 15 players on the UWSP roster scored as the top-ranked Pointers dismantled the Red Hawks 75-53 in nonconference action in its home opener.

"Point plays so well together as a team," Ripon coach Bob Gillespie said. "All I can do is compliment Stevens Point. Point gave us a lesson tonight."

Coming off a 24-point win over UW-La Crosse the night before, the Red Hawks (3-1) entertained thoughts of a monumental upset. With that in mind, the Red Hawks did their best to keep the Pointers' lethal 1-2 punch of Nick Bennett and Kalsow in check.

Gillespie can applaud his team for a job well done, as Kalsow and Bennett, who struggled through a 3-for-9 shooting night for 10 points, were each held well below their season averages.

"What we tried to do was not give up 60 points to those two kids," Gillespie said. "Our mind was willing, but our spirit was weak."

So Eric Maus, and the rest of the so-called role players, served notice that the Pointers are more than a two-player team.

Maus, a 6-foot-9 senior center, outhustled every Ripon player on the floor to chip in with 10 points, five assists and a steal.

Meanwhile, Jon Krull handled the heavy lifting with a game-high seven rebounds to go with eight points. Brian Bauer came off the bench to contribute seven points, hitting 3 of 4 shots from the field.

"I think we're all better off when we have more balance, because that makes it tougher to stop us," Maus said. "Coach (Jack Bennett) has stressed that from the start.

"And the thing about those two guys (Bennett and Kalsow) is they're great passers. When they get double-teamed, we have to make sure we find the open spots."

The Pointers (4-0) had a tough time shaking the Red Hawks until an 8-0 run to close out the opening half gave the Pointers a 32-18 lead at the break.

That would be the beginning of the end for Ripon.

A 19-2 spurt early in the second half sent UWSP well on its way to its 39th straight regular-season win over a nonconference opponent. The advantage grew to as much as 31 points at 74-43 with 2:01 remaining.

"I was anxious to see how much energy and fire we would come out with at home," Bennett said. "I thought the way we played is the way the game should be played."

The victory was important for the Pointers coach on a number of fronts.

Bennett passed his brother Dick for second place on the all-time coaches win list at the school. He now has 175, behind only Hale Quandt.

In addition, Ripon is the alma mater of Jack Bennett, who graduated from the school in 1971. He was offered the coaching job at Ripon in 1980 but turned it down. Gillespie, who coached at Wausau Newman at the time, eventually landed the Red Hawks position.

"The school was very good to me and means a lot to my family. It's the home of my wife," Jack Bennett said. "To be honest, I wanted us to look good against them. I have a lot of respect for their coach and program."

POINTERS 75, RED HAWKS 53

RIPON COLLEGE (53) - Bo Johnson 2-8 2-2 7, Wally DeVries 2-5 1-1 5, Tom Becker 4-6 4-4 14, Jered Massen 1-3 2-2 5, David McMullen 2-9 0-0 5, Jonathan Murphy 2-3 0-0 5, Paul Wise 2-4 0-0 5, Brian Schmitting 3-4 1-3 7. Totals 18-44 10-12 53.

UW-STEVENS POINT (75) - Nick Bennett 3-9 2-2 10, Jason Kalsow 5-10 3-4 14, Eric Maus 5-7 0-0 10, Tamaris Relerford 1-2 0-0 3, Jon Krull 3-6 0-0 8, Shawn Lee 1-2 0-0 3, Brett Hirsch 2-2 0-0 4, Brad Kalsow 0-2 2-2 2, Steve Hicklin 2-2 0-0 5, Kyle Grusczynski 2-4 0-0 5, Cory Krautkramer 0-2 0-0 0, Matt Bouche 0-1 0-0 0, Brian Bauer 3-4 0-0 7, Mike Prey 0-1 1-2 1, Gbenga Awe 1-1 1-2 3. Totals 28-55 9-12 75.

Ripon	18	35	- 53
UW-Stevens Point	32	43	- 75

3-point goals: Ripon 7-20 (Johnson 1-6, Becker 2-2, Massen 1-3, McMullen 1-4, Murphy 1-2, Wise 1-3), Stevens Point 10-20 (Bennett 2-7, J. Kalsow 1-2, Relerford 1-2, Krull 2-2, Lee 1-1, B. Kalsow 0-1, Hicklin 1-1, Grusczynski 1-2, Krautkramer 0-1, Bauer 1-1). Total fouls: Ripon 14, Stevens Point 10. Fouled out: none. Rebounds: Ripon 22 (Schmitting 5), Stevens Point 31 (Krull 7). Turnovers: Ripon 15, Stevens Point 10. Att.-1,578.

Top: Possessing great athleticism and a wide wing span on defense, Grusczynski causes all kinds of headaches for opposing teams.

Below: Kyle Grusczynski shoots a three-pointer against Marquette.

TOM CHARLESWORTH

PHOTO COURTESY OF UWSP SPORTS INFORMATION OFFICE

FEATURE
KYLE GRUSCZYNSKI

Grusczynski finds happiness on and off the court

By Scott Williams

Kyle Grusczynski has a lot of reasons to be happy these days.

His University of Wisconsin-Stevens Point men's basketball team is in the hunt for a second straight NCAA Division III national championship.

Grusczynski, a 6-foot-6 senior, already owns one ring. But it's an engagement ring he gave to his fiancee, Megan Stadler, that really has him smiling.

"To be able to come home to her is a huge relief. She's there to listen to me and give me advice," said Grusczynski, who will tie the knot with Stadler on June 3, 2006. "When I have a bad day, she let's me vent to her."

There was a time not so long ago when Grusczynski was not a very happy person. In reality, it was much worse. Grusczynski was suffering from depression. He was miserable his freshman year at the University of Wisconsin after accepting a Division I basketball scholarship from the Badgers.

Basketball was no longer fun, and felt more like a job. Grusczynski felt out of place on a campus with 40,000 students. Basketball and school were all-consuming. There was no time for a social life.

"Actually, it started at the end of my senior year," Grusczynski said. "It (the depression) just came on. It was a real struggle for about a month. I wasn't sleeping. At Madison, I never felt like myself. I was constantly in the gym, class or study table. Friends would want to go out and I was like, 'Man, I'm tired.' There was not any 'Me time.'"

Grusczynski left the basketball team after the first semester but remained enrolled at the university.

The time spent away from the court taught him how much basketball meant to him. Grusczynski missed the game and had the desire to start playing again.

After taking some looks at Eau Claire and Oshkosh, Grusczynski transferred to Stevens Point because of its proximity to his hometown of Seymour.

"I think Kyle found himself here," Pointer coach Jack Bennett said. "It's been documented that he battles with depression. He feels better about himself and it certainly helps to have basketball."

Grusczynski has served as the team's Mr. Versatility in his three years with the program. At any given point in his Pointer career, the lanky and athletic player has seen time at any of four positions. About the only spot to elude him is the pivot. And chances are, if called upon, Grusczynski would equate himself just fine at center, too.

"Obviously, Kyle has some skills to have Wisconsin offer him a scholarship," Bennett said. "But I think he feels more relaxed and comfortable showing his aggressive side coming off the bench. Plus, he gives us a little better athlete at some positions when he comes in."

The chance to play point guard this season has been especially satisfying for Grusczynski. Unselfish by

Above: Grusczynski began his career as a scholarship player at the University of Wisconsin before transferring to UWSP and winning two national titles.

nature, he enjoys every second he spends running the offense, sometimes out of necessity (injuries to Tamaris Relerford and Shawn Lee), but often by design.

"When I was little, I used to always bug my dad to let me play point guard," Grusczynski said. "I've been this tall since about sixth grade, so he was like. 'Just get down low.' I gradually got on his nerves enough for him to give in and I handled myself pretty well. My perimeter game and ball-handling are second nature now."

It would only have been natural for someone moving from a Division I program to the Division III level to want to take over. Nothing could be further from the truth for Grusczynski, who melded with his UWSP teammates. No role on the team was above him. There was never any pouting or tantrums when plays weren't designed for him.

He only has 11 starts during his Pointer career, but the importance of his role as the quintessential sixth-man on the team can't be dismissed or overestimated.

"I just want to go out and contribute however I can," Grusczynski said. "Everyone has a competitive nature and wants to be out there at crunch time. But everyone on this team just wants to win. They never tried to pigeon-hole me into one position or role. There was never any pressure to score so many points or do this or do this."

His contributions to the team aren't limited to the offensive end.

Grusczynski, who looks to have a wing span of a player twice his height, is out front in the Pointers' vaunted 3-2 or 1-3-1 zone defense, causing all sorts of headaches. If he's not making it tough for someone to shoot over him, Grusczynski is getting his hand on the ball for deflections or steals.

"What Kyle has is a lot of natural length and quickness," Bennett said.

Life and basketball are pretty sweet right now for Grusczynski.

Still, there are days when Grusczynski feels a little down and wrestles with depression. Those days are far less common and much less frequent, however.

"Sometimes with the stress of school and basketball, I'll feel down for a couple of days," Grusczynski said. "But it's nothing like it used to be."

Nothing another national championship and a pending marriage can't cure.

WISCONSIN
INTERCOLLEGIATE ATHLETIC CONFERENCE

UWSP Defeats Platteville in WIAC Opener

By Scott Williams

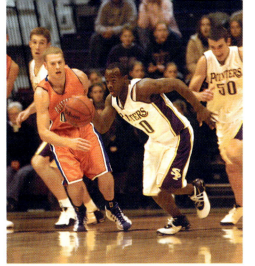

DOUG WOJCIK

Above: Tamaris Relerford leads the break against UW-Platteville.

Below: Jason Kalsow gets a wide open look thanks to a screen set by his brother Brad.

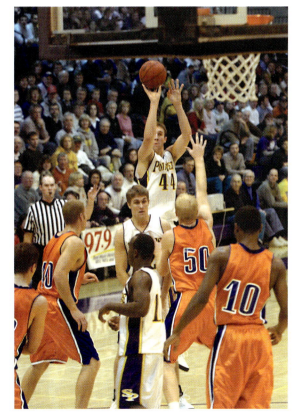

DOUG WOJCIK

Tamaris Relerford felt like he had just gone 12 rounds in the ring with Lennox Lewis.

The senior point guard for the University of Wisconsin-Stevens Point men's basketball team spent Tuesday night running into, through and around screens. Just for good measure, Relerford left some skin on the court, diving after loose balls.

Relerford sacrificed his body all over the court as the Pointers toughed out a 55-44 victory over a determined UW-Platteville team at the Quandt Fieldhouse.

The game was the Wisconsin Intercollegiate Athletic Conference opener for both teams.

Relerford was ready to go another 12 rounds, although some elbow pads and mouth guards could come in handy.

"You find yourself feeling like a pinball out there with all the screens," said Relerford, who spent the entire night guarding Pioneer standout and leading scorer Brad Reitzner. "I played football in high school, so I like all that contact.

"Reitzner is like the head of that team. You take the head away and the whole team struggles."

All that was missing was the guillotine.

Reitzner, a 6-foot-1 senior, entered Tuesday averaging 15 points a game and was a first team all-WIAC selection last season.

But the Platteville guard barely had enough room to breathe, let alone find enough open space to get his shot off. The result was a 2-for-11 shooting performance by Reitzner and a nine-point night.

Brandon Temperly and Sean Krause did their best to pick up the slack with 10 points apiece. However, the Pioneers (3-3, 0-1 WIAC) shot just 32.7 percent.

The take-no-prisoners attitude displayed by Relerford set the tone for the Pointers (5-0, 1-0 WIAC).

"We received an inspirational effort from Tamaris. That was one of the most intense and one of the greatest hustle performances I've seen," said UWSP coach Jack Bennett, whose team has won 14 straight.

Relerford threw himself a couple bones on the offensive end, sinking three of five shots from beyond the arc for nine points.

The serious scoring part of the night was left up to Mr. Reliable - better known as Jason Kalsow.

The senior forward from Huntley, Ill. employed a combination of post moves and mid-range jump shots to score a game-high 22 points. He also shared rebounding honors with Eric Maus at eight boards.

Kalsow was about the only bright spot for either team on offense.

"Any time you get jump-started in this league you have to be happy. You don't ask how and it's not always going to be smooth," said Bennett. "We hung in there and took some real good shots from Platteville. We found a way to win."

Platteville managed to go the final 10:06 of the first half without a field goal, but still only trailed 25-15 at intermission.

A 7-0 run to open the second half gave the Pointers plenty to think about. The game remained nip-and-tuck throughout the second half, with the Pioneers getting as close as three points on five different occasions.

"In all three games we lose it's pretty much been the same story. We get behind and can't quite get back. It's a matter of not being able to finish and convert our touches inside," Reitzner said.

Every time the Pioneers tried to land a haymaker, UWSP was there with a counterpunch to build the lead back up to seven or 10 points.

Jon Krull's 3-pointer from the left corner made it 52-43 with less than a minute left, and had the Pioneers loading up the covered wagons and heading home. It was his only basket of the night.

This was just the first in what Bennett is convinced will be a season full of tough, down-to-the-wire games.

"Those are battles out there. The kind you have to grind out," Bennett said. "I love to win and the players love to win. It doesn't matter if it's neatly packaged or a blue collar down and dirty win."

Left to Right:
- Tamaris Relerford goes up for a layup.
- Brad Kalsow grabs an offensive rebound against the Pioneers.
- Jason Kalsow up for two of his game-high 22 points.

POINTERS 55, PIONEERS 44

UW-PLATTEVILLE (44) - Brandon Temperly 3-10 2-2 9, Mark Gossens 5-7 0-0 10, Jeff Skemp 1-6 0-0 2, Brad Reitzner 2-11 3-4 9, Sean Krause 3-7 3-3 10, LeVon Crawford 2-5 0-0 4, Kendall Syse 0-1 0-0 0, Branden Jung 0-1 0-0 0, Josh Wesley 0-1 0-0 0. Totals 16-49 8-9 44.

UW-STEVENS POINT (55) - Nick Bennett 4-12 0-0 9, Jason Kalsow 9-16 3-4 22, Eric Maus 2-5 4-4 8, Tamaris Relerford 3-6 0-0 9, Jon Krull 1-4 0-0 3, Brad Kalsow 2-3 0-0 4, Kyle Grusczynski 0-1 0-0 0, Brian Bauer 0-1 0-0 0. Totals 21-48 7-8 55.

UW-Platteville	15	29	- 44
UW-Stevens Point	25	30	- 55

3-point goals: Platteville 4-10 (Temperly 1-2, Reitzner 2-6, Krause 1-1, Syse 0-1), Stevens Point 6-19 (Bennett 1-7, J. Kalsow 1-3, Relerford 3-5, Krull 1-3, Grusczynski 0-1). Total fouls: Platteville 12, Stevens Point 13. Fouled out: none. Rebounds: Platteville 29 (Temperly, Skemp 6), Stevens Point 33 (J. Kalsow, Maus 8). Turnovers: Platteville 10, Stevens Point 10. Att. - 1,532.

DOUG WOJCIK

DOUG WOJCIK

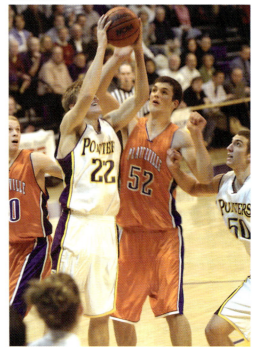

DOUG WOJCIK

Top: Head Coach Jack Bennett asks for an explanation from the referee during the Pointers 71-50 victory over UW-Eau Claire.

Below: Jason Kalsow goes up for a block during first half action.

PHOTO COURTESY OF LAYNE PITT

WISCONSIN
INTERCOLLEGIATE ATHLETIC CONFERENCE

UWSP wins with second-half spurt

By Scott Williams

EAU CLAIRE - The University of Wisconsin-Stevens Point men are proving the basketball court is one venue where the defense never rests.

Top-ranked UWSP held UW-Eau Claire to 19 points in the second half and went on to rout the Blugolds 71-50 at Zorn Arena on Saturday.

Through two Wisconsin Intercollegiate Athletic Conference games, the Pointers have given up an average of just 47 points. Eau Claire shot a cool 37.5 percent.

Not coincidentally, UWSP is 2-0 in the conference.

What made Saturday's defensive performance even more impressive was that UWSP shut down the Blugolds without the service of 6-foot-9 center Eric Maus, who went down with a sprained ankle in the first half.

"Not having Eric was a concern from a defensive standpoint," Pointer coach Jack Bennett said. "I'm as proud of our second half as anything we've done."

The Pointers (6-0) also found their offensive rhythm in Eau Claire.

After struggling from the field in recent games, UWSP shot 56.3 percent from the field, including a sizzling 61.5 percent in the second half.

Stuck in a 31-31 tie at halftime, the Pointers, behind All-American candidate Jason Kalsow, outscored Eau Claire 40-19 over the final 20 minutes.

A 10-0 run early in the second half put the Pointers on their way.

Kalsow finished with 23 points and moved closer to breaking the school's all-time career scoring record. Joining him in double figures were Jon Krull with 13 points, while Nick Bennett added 11.

"I thought we were a little out-toughed in the first half," Bennett said. "We needed to stem that or it was going to turn into one of those games that goes down to the wire.

"We went inside, and not just to one guy. We feel we have the ability to flash the post with a number of different people. Jason, Jon Krull and even Nick did some nice things down there."

The Pointers had 38 points in the paint compared to 14 for the Blugolds (3-3 1-1 WIAC).

PHOTO COURTESY OF LAYNE PITT

Dan Archambault and Casey Drake, scored 15 and 14 points, respectively, to pace the Blugolds.

Much of the credit for slowing down Drake in the second half should be heaped in the lap of senior UWSP guard Tamaris Relerford, who is quickly establishing himself as a stopper in the backcourt.

"Tamaris has turned in two real gutsy performances now the last two (WIAC) games," Bennett said. "He's playing as mature and as good as he has in our program."

Top: Jason Kalsow drives baseline against the Blugolds.

Right: Senior Eric Maus works for rebound position.

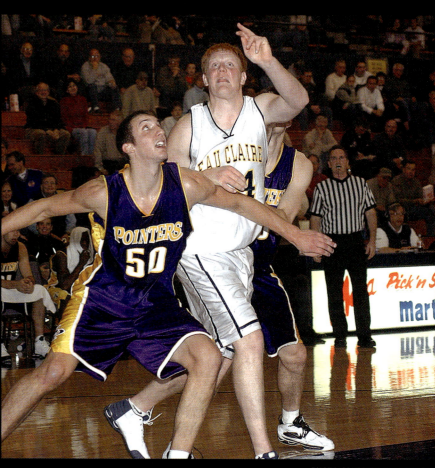

POINTERS 71, BLUGOLDS 50

UW-STEVENS POINT (71) - Tamaris Relerford 3-5 0-0 9, Nick Bennett 4-8 1-1 11, Jon Krull 6-6 1-1 13, Jason Kalsow 9-16 5-8 23; Eric Maus 1-2 1-2 3, Brett Hirsch 0-1 1-3 1, Brad Kalsow 2-3 0-1 6, Steve Hicklin 1-1 0-0 2, Kyle Grusczynski 1-1 0-0 3, Cory Krautkramer 0-2 0-0 0, Brian Bauer 0-1 0-0 0, Gbenga Awe 0-2 0-0 0. Totals 27-48 9-16 71.

UW-EAU CLAIRE (50) - Casey Drake 5-12 3-5 14, Dan Archambault 6-13 1-1 15, Will Jefferson 3-8 0-0 8, Dan Beyer 2-3 2-4 6, Tyler Birkel 1-4 1-3 3, Colin Walsh 0-3 0-0 0, Kale Proksch 1-2 2-2 4, Chad Honl 0-1 0-0 0, Marshall Watry 0-1 0-0 0, Buck Smith 0-1 0-0 0. Totals 18-48 9-15 50.

UW-Stevens Point 31 40 - 71
UW-Eau Claire   31 19 - 50

3-point goals: Stevens Point 8-16 (Relerford 3-5, Bennett 2-6, J. Kalsow 0-1, B. Kalsow 2-3, Grusczynski 1-1), Eau Claire 5-15 (Drake 1-4, Archambault 2-2, Jefferson 2-5, Beyer 0-1, Walsh 0-2, Watry 0-1). Total fouls: Stevens Point 16, Eau Claire 17. Fouled out: none. Rebounds: Stevens Point 34 (J. Kalsow 5), Eau Claire 27 (Proksch 7). Turnovers: Stevens Point 6, Eau Claire 6. Att. - 1,700.

PHOTO COURTESY OF LAYNE PITT

WISCONSIN
INTERCOLLEGIATE ATHLETIC CONFERENCE

Pointers defense stifles UW-River Falls

By Scott Williams

RIVER FALLS—UW-River Falls missed eight of its first nine shots on Tuesday night. It was just a sign of things to come all night long for the Falcons.

UW-Stevens Point held the Falcons to just 14 first half points and cruised to a 65-50 victory at the Karges Center in River Falls, improving to 7-0 overall and 3-0 in the WIAC.

UW-River Falls shot just 19.2 percent in the first half, going scoreless over a span of 7:26 as the Pointers went on a 12-0 run to eventually take a 29-14 halftime lead. UW-Stevens Point used another run in the second half, going on a 13-3 spurt to push the lead to 52-26 with seven minutes left.

UW-River Falls finished the game at 32.1 percent from the field, including just 23.1 percent from three-point range. Dan Torrez had 14 of his team-high 16 points in the second half for UW-River Falls, which fell to 3-3 overall and 0-2 in the WIAC.

The Pointers had 12 different players score with Jason Kalsow leading the way with 17 points, nine rebounds and five assists. Nick Bennett added 16 points and freshman Gbenga Awe tallied a career-high six points while playing 16 minutes in place of injured center Eric Maus, who had his streak snapped of having played in all 95 career games. Tamaris Relerford also knocked down two three-pointers to finish with six points.

POINTERS 65, UW-RIVER FALLS 50

UW-Stevens Point (65)--Relerford, Tamaris 2-3 0-0 6, Bennett, Nick 6-12 2-2 16, Krull, Jon 1-2 0-0 2, Bauer, Brian 1-3 0-0 3, Kalsow, Jason 6-10 3-4 17, Lee, Shawn 0-1 2-2 2, Hirsch, Brett 1-2 0-0 2, Kalsow, Brad 0-0 2-2 2, Hicklin, Steve 1-2 1-2 3, Grusczynski, Kyle 1-5 0-0 3, Krautkramer, Cory 0-0 0-0 0, Bouche, Matt 0-0 0-0 0, Prey, Mike 1-1 1-2 3, Leahy, Zach 0-0 0-0 0, Awe, Gbenga 3-5 0-4 6

UW-River Falls (50)--Holt, Jeff 1-6 0-0 2, Thompson, Ryan 2-7 1-2 6, Hoeg, Hans 3-12 4-4 11, Marchand, Hector 0-1 0-0 0, Coffman, Mitch 1-4 0-0 2, Kossoris, Eric 3-8 0-0 8, Hall, Nick 0-1 0-0 0, Torrez, Dan 6-13 2-3 16, Maas, Alex 0-0 0-0 0, Kelly, Scott 0-0 0-0 0, Lucarevic, Muris 1-1 3-6 5

UW-Stevens Point	29	36	- 65
UW-River Falls	14	36	- 50

3-point goals: Stevens Point 8-19 (Relerford 2-2, Bennett 2-6, J. Kalsow 2-2, Bauer 1-2, Grusczynski 1-4, Krull 0-1, Lee 0-1, Hicklin 0-1), River Falls 6-26. **Total fouls:** Stevens Point 13, River Falls 15. **Fouled out:** none. **Rebounds:** Stevens Point 38 (J. Kalsow 9), River Falls 28 (Coffman 6). **Turnovers:** Stevens Point 11, River Falls 7. **Att.** - 366.

WISCONSIN
INTERCOLLEGIATE ATHLETIC CONFERENCE

Pointers' Bennett sets school record for wins

By Jacey Zembal

STEVENS POINT - Jack Bennett's achievement Saturday was something after which courts or gymnasiums are named.

The University of Wisconsin-Stevens Point men's basketball coach set the school's all-time record for most wins with 179, surpassing Hale Quandt.

UWSP shot lights out in the second half (77.8 percent), especially from 3-point range to defeat UW-Stout 75-52. The Pointers, who are ranked No. 1 in Division III, took over sole possession of first place in the WIAC (8-0 overall, 4-0 conference).

Bennett might have to settle for the Bennett name residing on the court, since the Pointers play in Quandt Fieldhouse.

"That one will be up to the powers-to-be," Bennett said jokingly. "I thanked the team afterwards and got emotional about it. They are a wonderful group."

Bennett (179-53 record) credits past UWSP coaches and his past and current assistant coaches for the milestone.

"When I took the job nine years ago, (I never thought) that I would last this long to have a shot at the record," Bennett said. "The reason I've been able to stay is because I have great young men, on and off the floor."

Nick Bennett, Jack's son, scored a game-high 22 points to lead the Pointers, who extended their winning streak to 17 games, the second longest in school history.

"It's special and it is great to be a part of him setting the record," Nick Bennett said. "It's a tribute to all the players who have played for him over the years. This isn't a one-game thing, as it is a lifetime of effort."

Coach Bennett took a low profile when it came to his impending record.

"It wasn't surprising to me that he didn't say anything, but I knew it was coming up," Nick Bennett said. "Maybe, one day they can have a co-court with Dick Bennett and Jack Bennett court. If they ever do that, it would be awesome."

Dick Bennett, Jack's brother who now coaches at Washington State, also coached the Pointers.

After shooting 22.7-percent from the field in the first half, the Pointers needed someone to emerge. Enter Kyle Grusczynski, who

> "It's special and it is great to be a part of him setting the record. It's a tribute to all the players who have played for him over the years."
> —*Nick Bennett*

Below: Head Coach Jack Bennett can't believe the call.

DOUG WOJCIK

Left: Senior John Gleich follows the action against Stout.

Right: Steve Hicklin drives to the hoop.

DOUG WOJCIK

POINTERS 75, BLUE DEVILS 52

UW-Stout (52): Kailus Coleman 1-5 0-0 2, Brian Buck 2-6 0-1 4, Terry Farmer 1-2 2-2 4, Adam Chandler 4-13 1-2 9, Ryan Stangl 1-9 2-2 5, Anthony Stotts 0-2 0-0 0, Jesse Huser 0-4 0-0 0, Nate Fern 0-1 1-2 1, Jason Clopton 0-0 0-2 0, Tyler Kazmierkoski 0-3 2-2 2, Greg Chaisson 3-7 1-2 8, Luke Loney 4-6 1-2 12, Eric Heisler 1-2 1-1 3, John Nonemacher 1-2 0-0 2, Jacob Nonemacher 0-2 0-0 0. FG: 18-64, 28.1%. FT: 11-18, 61.1%.

UW-Stevens Point (75): Nick Bennett 5-10 10-11 22, Jason Kalsow 2-6 7-7 11, Tamaris Relerford 1-6 0-0 3, Kyle Grusczynski 4-6 2-2 14, Jon Krull 3-5 6-8 13, Shawn Lee 2-2 2-2 7, Brett Hirsch 0-0 0-0 0, Brad Kalsow 0-2 0-0 0, Steve Hicklin 0-0 0-0 0, Cory Krautkramer 1-1 1-1 3, Brian Bauer 0-1 0-0 0, Mike Prey 0-0 0-0 0, Gbenga Awe 1-1 0-0 2, John Gleich 0-0 0-0 0. FG: 19-40, 47.5%. FT: 28-31, 90.3%.

UW-Stout	23	29	- 52
UW-Stevens Point	25	50	- 75

3-point goals: Stout 5-28, Stevens Point 9-21 (Bennett 2-5, Relerford 1-5, Krull 1-2, Lee 1-1, B. Kalsow 0-2, Grusczynski 4-5, Bauer 0-1). Total fouls: Stout 28, Stevens Point 10. Fouled out: Stout-Nonemacher. Rebounds: Stout 38 Stevens Point 36 (J. Kalsow 11). Turnovers: Stout 12, Stevens Point 11.

shot 4 of 5 from 3-point land and finished with 14 points. The senior needed a confidence boost because he has been struggling of late (3.3 points a game).

"To be honest, I was terrible shooting the ball in pre-game warm-ups," Grusczynski said. "For some reason the ball found me and I caught it with my feet ready and let it fly. It was really pure because none of them even hit the rim when they went it."

UW-Stout coach Eddie Andrist said there wasn't anything his team could do differently in the second half. The Blue Devils (4-3 overall, 3-1 WIAC) held the Pointers to 22.7-percent shooting in the first half.

"We talked at halftime about playing intense on defense and to stay with their shooters, but obviously, that didn't happen in the second half," Andrist said. "To give up 77-percent shooting in the second half is ridiculous. If there was a seventh grade team out there and they played UW-Stevens Point, they probably wouldn't give up 77-percent shooting."

UWSP doesn't play again until December 29, when they host Viterbo University. Coach Bennett was concerned about the long layoff at the beginning of the season, but now welcomes the prolonged break.

"We can practice the next upcoming week, but then give the kids off from December 18-25," coach Bennett said. "We've been very intense since the start of the year because we played Marquette University two weeks before the season started. I just want us to catch our breath emotionally and mentally. Plus, we have some injuries (Eric Maus) that need to heal."

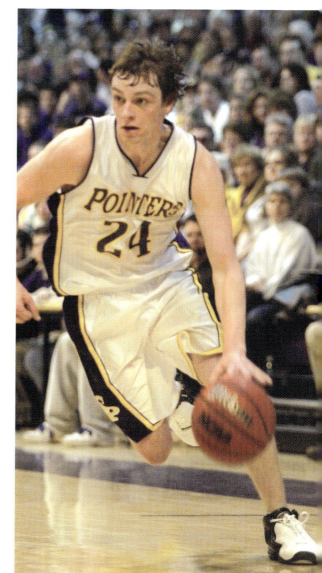

DOUG WOJCIK

SENTRY CLASSIC

Pointers still unbeaten

Below: Nick Bennett led the Pointers with 22 points against Viterbo.

By Scott Williams

Nick Bennett must have asked Santa Claus for good shooting this Christmas.

In fact, Jolly Old St. Nick must've had the entire University of Wisconsin-Stevens Point men's basketball team on his list of those who were nice.

UWSP came out on fire and Viterbo College never stood a chance in a blistering 86-54 victory for the top-ranked Pointers at the Quandt Fieldhouse in the 33rd annual Sentry Holiday Classic on Wednesday night.

Bennett found his shooting touch against the V-Hawks, drilling five of his six attempts from 3-point range on the way to 17 first-half points. By that time, the game was for the most part over as the Pointers built an insurmountable 46-23 lead.

Nick Bennett finished with a team-high 22 points.

"You won't see a better shooting performance at any level," UWSP coach Jack Bennett said, adding to his school record victory total which now stands at 180. "We were hitting on all cylinders tonight, and when we do that we're a pretty decent team.

"I thought Nick really ignited us. Is it contagious? Yes. When Nick starts it then it helps guys like Brad Kalsow off the bench. We've got some good shooters."

No one has a better reputation for being able to shoot the lights out than Nick Bennett.

But the senior forward/guard has seen his long distance shot go wary through the first eight games of the season. Bennett came into the Sentry Classic shooting 35 percent from behind the arc.

"We're winning, so I don't think about how I'm doing. We're still 9-0. If we're losing, then it might be different," said Nick Bennett. "It's definitely nice to get back in the swing of things and shoot the ball well."

Nick Bennett wasn't the only Pointer who got a hot hand for Christmas.

The shooting numbers in the opening 20 minutes were mind-boggling. UWSP shot a blistering 70 percent from the field, including an unconscionable 77 percent (10-for-13) from 3-point land.

Brad Kalsow came off the bench to drain all three of his treys and connect on four 3-pointers in all to wind up with 12 points. Shawn Lee made his only shot from behind the arc. Not to be left out, Jason Kalsow added a 3-pointer and then went inside to

DOUG WOJCIK

finish the half with 12 of his game total of 17 points.

Not exactly the kind of memories Viterbo coach Wayne Wagner wanted on his latest trip to Quandt.

"They shot great in the first half. What makes them such a good team is that they work themselves into position to get good looks," said Wagner, who served as an assistant coach under Jack Bennett from 1997-99. "It wasn't just Bennett. Everybody got their chance and made it. (Brad) Kalsow came in off the bench and shot lights out. There is not much you can do at that point."

Jeremy Fradette paced the V-Hawks (8-8) with 12 points, while Greg Kumlien contributed 11 points off the bench.

Part of the reason the Pointers came out in top form, according to coach Bennett, is they didn't take Viterbo lightly.

"This was a different script than the last couple times we've played them. Usually we've traded punches in the first half and then we get control in the second," coach Bennett said. "I think part of our alertness and the way we came out was because we respected them."

Left: Tamaris Relerford brings the ball up against Viterbo.

DOUG WOJCIK

POINTERS 86, V-HAWKS 54

VITERBO (54) - Justin Kirking 1-3 2-2 4, Jeremy Fradette 6-10 0-0 12, Kyle Hinbes 2-7 1-1 6, Vince Ruger 1-8 2-2 5, Aaron Bennet 3-5 0-0 7, Greg Kumlien 3-4 4-5 11, Rob Sebion 0-0 1-2 1, Travis Bassett 0-3 2-2 2, Tim Porterfield 1-6 0-0 3, B.J. Reber 1-5 1-2 3. Totals 18-51 13-16 54.

UW-STEVENS POINT (86) - Nick Bennett 7-12 2-2 22, Jason Kalsow 6-9 4-4 17, Mike Prey 1-2 2-4 4, Tamaris Relerford 1-3 1-1 3, Jon Krull 2-4 0-0 4, Shawn Lee 1-1 4-4 7, Brett Hirsch 1-2 1-2 3, Brad Kalsow 4-4 0-0 12, Steve Hicklin 2-2 0-0 5, Cory Krautkramer 0-3 2-2 2, Matt Bouche 1-2 0-0 2, Eric Maus 2-4 0-0 4, Gbenga Awe 0-1 1-2 1. Totals 28-49 17-21 86.

Viterbo	23	31	- 54
UW-Stevens Point	46	40	- 86

3-point goals: Viterbo 5-17 (Hines 1-4, Ruger 1-6, Bennet 1-2, Kumlien 1-2, Porterfield 1-3), UWSP 13-20 (Bennett 6-10, J. Kalsow 1-2, Relerford 0-2, Lee 1-1, B. Kalsow 4-4, Hicklin 1-1). Total fouls: Viterbo 20, UWSP 19. Fouled out: Awe. Rebounds: Viterbo 22 (Fradette 5), UWSP 36 (J. Kalsow 6). Turnovers: Viterbo 11, UWSP 13. Att. - 1,820.

SENTRY CLASSIC

Krull has hot hand in Pointers win

By Scott Williams

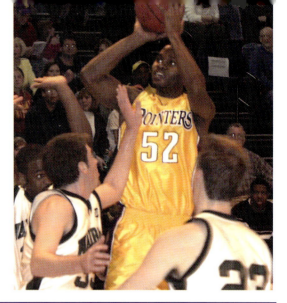

Right: Gbenga Awe shoots a baseline jumper in the Pointers Sentry Classic win over Wisconsin Lutheran.

TOM KUJAWSKI

Jon Krull isn't big on the grand entrance. Truth be told, he's content to operate in anonymity during most University of Wisconsin-Stevens Point men's basketball games.

So it only seemed fitting that Krull used the back door to make a major impact Thursday night in the finale of the 33rd annual Sentry Classic.

Krull scored a season-high 19 points to lead three players in double figures as the top-ranked Pointers crushed Wisconsin Lutheran College 82-42 at the Quandt Fieldhouse.

The sophomore from Marshall came into the game averaging 7.4 points a game.

"It's all based on our offense. We use a five-man motion," said Krull of his offensive explosion. "They were overplaying the passing lanes hard and I'm the designated cutter in the offense. It leaves a lot open for me."

Krull was a factor right from the start - which is a news bulletin in itself. For one reason or another, points have been tough for Krull to come by in the opening halves of games this season. That certainly wasn't the case against Wisconsin Lutheran, which watched Krull shred their defense for 10 first-half points - nearly matching his total in the opening halves of the first nine games.

With Krull padding his numbers with lay-up after lay-up, and Jason Kalsow and Nick Bennett up to their usual tricks with 17 and 14 points, respectively, UWSP (10-0) was able to build a commanding 45-18 lead at halftime. Krull's own personal lay-up drill was the subject of some good-natured ribbing from his teammates who were wondering if he could make a shot outside 5 feet.

"Things just opened up for me. More of my offense has been coming inside this season with post ups," Krull said. "It just gives us another offensive weapon we can bring to the table."

Even the referees felt this one was over at halftime. The start of the second half was delayed for several minutes as the officials were tardy returning to the court. All that remained to be seen was just how large the final margin of victory would become.

The proverbial garbage time began with 12 minutes left. UWSP enjoyed its biggest lead of 43 points at 80-37 with 1:18 remaining in regulation.

"We hold them to a standard. We try to play Pointer basketball every second we're on the court," UWSP coach Jack Bennett said. "We beat two goods teams the last two nights. I'm not saying they're world-beaters, but they'll do well in the leagues. We have the potential to make good teams look bad."

It was the 41st straight regular season nonconference win for the Pointers, who extended their winning streak to 19 over the past two seasons. The Pointers did it with a stingy defense and an unselfish and pinpoint passing display that would make the Harlem Globetrotters green with envy.

Through 10 games, UWSP has not allowed more than 59 points in a game and teams are shooting just 35 percent from the field. The Warriors (4-7) couldn't even live up to that unimpressive standard, connecting on just 16 of 64 field goal attempts - a frigid 25 percent.

"When I shook hands with their coach (Edward Noon) after the game the first thing he said was, 'Your defense is not getting enough cred-it' said coach Bennett. "I do feel our defense is better than it's been."

It also would be hard to imagine a better passing team. Of the 33 field goals UWSP made in the game 20 came on the end of assists. As a result, the Pointers piled up easy baskets which might help explain why they continued their torrid shooting pace with a 58 percent effort from the field Thursday. That performance came on the heels of a 70 percent outing, and the point man on the exquisite passing exhibition was none other than Jason Kalsow. The 6-foot-7 senior center dished out a team-high six assists and set an example of what unselfish play can do for a team.

"This is a team that really looks for one another," coach Bennett said. "And when you hold teams in the 30s, 40s and 50s in today's age of basketball that's pretty good."

POINTERS 82, WARRIORS 42

WISCONSIN LUTHERAN (42) - B.J. Miller 3-6 0-0 6, Brian Hagel 2-6 0-0 5, Lewis Jiles 1-4 0-0 2, Adam Markham 0-1 0-0 0, Kevin Christensen 4-22 3-4 12, Stefan Spath 0-6 0-0 0, Brandon Markham 0-0 1-2 1, Marcus Zondag 0-0 1-2 1, Andrew Kimball 1-1 0-0 2, Nate Sorum 0-5 0-0 0, Mo Wilburn 0-1 0-0 0, Nick Aiello 1-2 1-1 3, Brandon Mattox 1-2 0-0 2, Matt Dunlop 0-2 1-2 1, Nathan Zondag 3-6 1-1 7. Totals 16-64 8-12 42.

UW-STEVENS POINT (82) - Nick Bennett 6-9 0-0 14, Jason Kalsow 7-11 3-3 17, Tamaris Relerford 1-3 2-2 5, Kyle Grusczynski 1-2 0-1 2, Jon Krull 8-9 3-3 19, Shawn Lee 0-1 0-0 0, Brett Hirsch 2-3 1-4 5, Brad Kalsow 3-6 0-0 6, Steve Hicklin 0-2 2-4 2, Cory Krautkramer 0-1 0-1 0, Matt Bouche 1-1 1-1 3, Brian Bauer 2-2 0-0 5, Mike Prey 1-2 0-0 2, Gbenga Awe 1-5 0-0 2. Totals 33-57 12-19 82.

Wisconsin Lutheran	18	24	- 42
UW-Stevens Point	45	37	- 82

3-point goals: Wisconsin Lutheran 2-15 (Miller 0-1, Hagel 1-3, Jiles 0-1, A. Markham 0-1, Christensen 1-6, Spath 0-1, Aiello 0-1, Mattox 0-1), UWSP 4-14 (Bennett 2-4, Relerford 1-3, Grusczynski 0-1, Lee 0-1, B. Kalsow 0-2, Hicklin 0-2, Bauer 1-1). Total fouls: Wisconsin Lutheran 20, UWSP 13. Fouled out: none. Rebounds: Wisconsin Lutheran 28 (Spath, Sorum 5), UWSP 48 (J. Kalsow 9). Turnovers: Wisconsin Lutheran 12, UWSP 14.

FEATURE
ERIC MAUS
Center of Activity

By Scott Williams

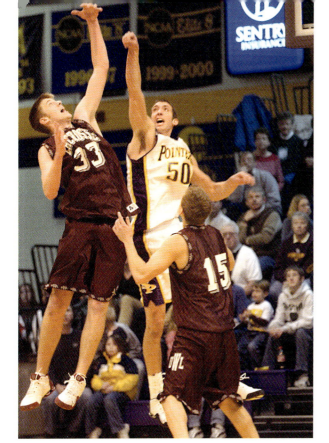

Top: Senior Eric Maus blocks a shot against La Crosse.

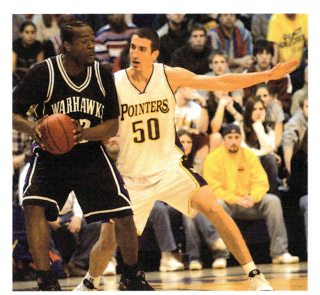

Below: Head Coach Jack Bennett called Maus "the Pointers best defender".

You might as well call him "The Quiet Assassin." More often than not he comes to the rescue of teammates who have been beaten on defense.

He's more formerly known as Eric Maus, a 6-foot-9 senior center on the University of Wisconsin-Stevens Point men's basketball team.

Off the court, it would be hard to imagine a nicer, more humble, soft-spoken person than the Green Bay native.

Once he laces up his sneakers and puts on his purple and gold Pointer uniform, however, Maus makes a lot of noise in ways that often go unnoticed.

"I wish I knew who coined the phrase, 'Still waters run deep.' He's a quiet and painfully shy guy, but underneath it all is a very deep player who knows how to think the game," UWSP coach Jack Bennett said. "I don't look at Eric so much as an unsung hero for us. He's done enough things where he's made a mark on this program. He doesn't go out seeking attention."

Given a choice, Maus would be completely content to come to practice, play the games and quietly slip into the background.

There was a time when Maus wasn't sure he wanted or could be part of any Division III program. As a freshman, he wrestled with doubts about whether he had the ability and make-up to contribute to the Pointer program.

"I didn't know if I could make it at this level," Maus said. "Coach talked to me and convinced me to give it a try. So I went to practice and I've been with the team ever since."

No one is happier he did than Bennett. Coaches tend to appreciate what players like Maus bring to the court more than the casual basketball fan. Maus plays basketball the way James Naismith intended when he invented the game: keep mistakes to a minimum and do whatever it takes to make the players around you, and ultimately the team, better.

"I would like to think I play pretty smart. I'm a pretty solid defender and I'm able to find the open man with a pass," said Maus, who received honorable mention to the Wisconsin Intercollegiate Athletic Conference all-conference team this season.

He was the third leading scorer on his high school team at Green Bay Southwest, but that didn't stop Fox River Valley Conference coaches from voting Maus the league's Player of the Year.

Maus has never averaged more than 8.4 points or five rebounds a game in his college career. Yet, his contributions aren't lost on his teammates.

"He is the definition of a team basketball player," Pointer senior guard Nick Bennett said. "I've never heard him once say anything negative and he's the first to congratulate you when you do something well."

Maus has been an integral part of the Pointers' success over the past couple of years without any interest whatsoever in stuffing a stat sheet. He won't impress you with any rim-shaking dunks. If it's a dazzling display of drives, pull-up jumpers and behind-the-back passes you want, then Maus isn't the player for you.

Above: Pointer senior Eric Maus.

PHOTO COURTESY OF UWSP SPORTS INFORMATION OFFICE

"We've worked hard with Eric on his ability to finish near the basket. We have to beg him to dunk the ball in practice. He would rather go with the safe play and lay the ball in," Bennett said.

Need someone to make a defensive stop with the game on the line, call No. 50. In search of a player to make an unselfish pass for an easy basket, or grab a loose ball or offensive rebound, Maus will do everything in his power to make it happen. He has earned the respect of the coaches he plays against as much as any 20 points a game scorer.

"Maus is a monster on defense. I don't think people realize the problems he causes with his length and ability to help out," Lawrence University coach John Tharp said after his team's 79-45 loss at the hands of UWSP in the second round of the NCAA Tournament last weekend.

Maus served a two-year internship coming off the bench as a freshman and sophomore at UWSP.

To listen to Maus, one would think the limited playing time he received those seasons was the equivalent of being a member of the Dream Team. Once he worked his way into the starting lineup as a junior, Maus was in basketball heaven.

"My first two years to be able to get some decent playing time was all I could possibly ask for. To be able to start the last two years, and be a part of some great teams, was the perfect situation for myself," Maus said.

Ask Maus to describe a perfect game in his eyes and he suggests the rather modest numbers of 10 points, 10 rebounds, seven or eight assists and shutting down the top scorer on the other team.

"I try to stay out of the spotlight. I think it's a combination of my personality and my abilities. I don't need to do those things on this team," Maus said. "I really don't mind not sticking out in a crowd - even at 6-9."

But no matter how hard he tries to avoid the spotlight, sometimes the limelight finds Maus, especially when you place him on a big stage.

During the Pointers' magical run to the national championship a year ago, Maus knocked down the winning shot with 5 seconds left in an 82-81 overtime win over Lawrence in the Elite Eight. The next weekend, Maus hit Jason Kalsow with a pass that led to the winning shot with less than 2 seconds left in regulation to give UWSP a 84-82 victory over Williams (Mass.) College in the national title game.

"I'm not sure anyone has been as valuable for us to become a cohesive team as he has been," coach Bennett said. "Eric might be very quiet, but he pays attention to detail on the court."

All in his own unassuming way.

WISCONSIN
INTERCOLLEGIATE ATHLETIC CONFERENCE

WARHAWKS KNOCK OFF POINTERS
Whitewater ends UWSP win streak at 19 games

By Scott Williams

Left: Jon Krull puts back an offensive rebound for two of his 15 points.

DOUG WOJCIK

WHITEWATER - Any talk of perfection for the University of Wisconsin-Stevens Point men's basketball team can stop. UW-Whitewater made sure of that Tuesday night.

The top-ranked Pointers watched their 19-game winning streak come to an end as Whitewater upended them 71-61 in Wisconsin Intercollegiate Athletic Conference action at Williams Arena. The loss leaves UWSP 10-1 overall and 4-1 in the WIAC, while the Warhawks move to respective marks of 10-3 and 2-3.

"We knew this was going to be a tough trip," Pointer coach Jack Bennett said. "We tried to put off the inevitable as long as we could. I guess now we've put everyone (in the WIAC) back in shooting range."

The Pointers had trouble finding their shooting eye, connecting on 37.1 percent of their field goal attempts on 23 for 62 shooting. Conversely, Whitewater was able to get off to a fast start, jumping out to a 27-15 lead with 7 minutes, 44 seconds left in the opening half by exploiting its superior quickness.

Angelo Griffin, who finished with 16 points, hurt the Pointers on the inside while Jeremy Manchester was a pain on the perimeter as the Warhawks became the first team to break 60 points against UWSP this season.

Manchester scored a team-high 18 points, including a 10-of-12 performance from the free throw line where the Warhawks held a 23-11 scoring edge. They also only turned the ball over six times.

"Our defense is not based so much on making teams turn the ball over. It's based on not putting people to the line very often," Bennett said. "It was due to a lack of anticipation and we fouled with the shot clock winding down in part due to their quickness."

UWSP gradually chipped away at the deficit and narrowed the margin to 32-26 at halftime. The gap continued to decrease until the Pointers took only their second lead of the game at 47-46 on a 3-pointer by Nick Bennett with 11:35 remaining in regulation. It would be the last time they would enjoy a lead in the game.

A pair of free throws by Mike Toellner with 5:15 left gave Whitewater the lead for good at 56-55. The Warhawks proceeded to secure the win at the free throw line.

"We played some good ball for spurts but we didn't sustain it like we've come to expect," Bennett said. "You can tell we were not that keen from the start. Sometimes you need to be knocked down. We need to bounce back and learn from this like we did from our losses last year."

POINTERS 63, WARHAWKS 71

UW-STEVENS POINT (63) - Tamaris Relerford 0-3 3-5 3, Nick Bennett 7-20 0-0 16, Jon Krull 6-10 3-5 15, Jason Kalsow 7-20 3-3 20, Eric Maus 0-1 0-0 0, Brad Kalsow 1-3 0-0 2, Kyle Grusczynski 2-5 2-3 7. Totals 23-62 11-16 63.

UW-WHITEWATER (71) - Giovanni Riley 2-5 0-1 4, Tony Miggins 2-5 0-0 5, Angelo Griffin 8-13 0-0 16, Melvin Williams 2-5 8-9 12, Mike Toellner 1-4 4-5 6, Rob Dixon 1-2 0-0 3, Craig Anderson 0-3 1-2 1, Jeremy Manchester 4-6 10-12 18, Jason Price 2-6 0-0 6, Rob Perry 0-2 0-0 0. Totals 22-51 23-29 71.

UW-Stevens Point	26	37	- 63
UW-Whitewater	32	39	- 71

3-points goals: Stevens Point 6-21 (Relerford 0-2, Bennett 2-8, Krull 0-1, J. Kalsow 3-6, B. Kalsow 0-1, Grusczynski 1-3), Whitewater 4-16 (Riler 0-2, Miggins 1-3, Williams 0-1, Dixon 1-2, Anderson 0-3, Manchester 0-1, Price 2-4). Total fouls: Stevens Point 22, Whitewater 15. Fouled out: none: Rebounds: Stevens Point 40 (J. Kalsow 8), Whitewater 30 (Griffin 8). Turnovers: Stevens Point 13, Whitewater 6. Att.-1,005.

THE SEASON
NONCONFERENCE

Pointers bounce back against Marian

By Scott Williams

FOND DU LAC - The University of Wisconsin-Stevens Point men's basketball team rebounded from Tuesday's loss at UW-Whitewater with a convincing 82-57 win at Marian College on Thursday.

The Pointers, the defending NCAA Division III national champions, opened the game by hitting six of first seven shots for a 15-10 lead and never looked back. After building a 40-28 halftime lead, UWSP (11-1, 4-1 Wisconsin Intercollegiate Athletic Conference) secured the win by hitting all six 3-point attempts in the second half.

Nick Bennett was the leading scorer for UWSP with 22 points while Jason Kalsow was one rebound away from a double-double (19 points, nine rebounds). Kalsow, a senior from Huntley, Ill., is currently seventh on the Pointers' all-time scoring list with 1,454 points. He is 52 points away from the next closest mark - 1,506 points by Brant Bailey from 1996-2000.

Jake Harmsen was the leading scorer for Marian (3-10) with nine points.

DOUG WOJCIK

Above: The Pointer bench saw plenty of action in the 82-57 victory over Marian.

POINTERS 82, MARIAN 57

UW-Stevens Point (82)--Relerford, Tamaris 2-3 0-0 6, Bennett, Nick 7-9 5-6 22, Krull, Jon 3-5 0-1 6, Kalsow, Jason 7-12 4-7 19, Maus, Eric 2-3 0-2 4, Lee, Shawn 2-3 0-0 6, Hirsch, Brett 2-3 0-0 4, Kalsow, Brad 2-2 0-0 6, Hicklin, Steve 0-3 0-0 0, Grusczynski, Kyle 2-2 0-0 5, Krautkramer, Cory 0-0 0-0 0, Bouche, Matt 0-1 0-0 0, Bauer, Brian 0-0 0-0 0, Prey, Mike 0-2 0-2 0, Awe, Gbenga 1-2 2-2 4

Marian (57)--Vogt, Nick 1-6 2-2 5, Wuest, Casey 4-9 0-1 8, Van Ess, Jordan 2-5 0-0 5, Redmond, Titus 3-6 1-2 7, Whitenack, David 3-10 0-0 6, Gray, Jason 0-0 2-2 2, Harmsen, Jake 2-7 4-5 9, Lofton, Jermaine 0-1 0-0 0, Kirby, Sean 0-1 0-0 0, Arndt, Derek 0-0 0-0 0, Gigiel, Greg 1-2 0-0 3, Wilhelmsen, Mike 0-0 0-0 0, Riley, LaQuandis 0-0 6-6 6, Godbolt, Alston 3-3 0-0 6

UW-Stevens Point	40	42	-	82
Marian	28	29	-	57

3-points goals: Stevens Point 11-15 (Relerford 2-3, Bennett 3-4, Krull 0-1, J. Kalsow 1-1, B. Kalsow 2-2, Grusczynski 1-1, Lee 2-2, Hicklin 0-1), Marian 4-12. Total fouls: Stevens Point 15, Marian 17. Fouled out: none: Rebounds: Stevens Point 33 (J. Kalsow 9), Marian 24. Turnovers: Stevens Point 14, Marian 13.

WISCONSIN
INTERCOLLEGIATE ATHLETIC CONFERENCE

UWSP serves frozen Eagles

By Nathan Vine

Left: Tamaris Relerford plays tight man-to-man defense against La Crosse. The Pointers held the Eagles to 13 total first half points.

STEVENS POINT JOURNAL STAFF

POINTERS 65, EAGLES 49

UW-La Crosse (49): Chris Ask 4-12 3-4 11, Aaron Stelzl 0-3 1-4 1, Joe Werner 5-11 2-2 12, Chris Fegrebbach 4-10 0-0 11, Josh Hall 1-3 2-3 5, Dan Borchard 0-1 0-0 0, Marcus Conigliaro 0-1 0-0 0, Andrew Huss 0-1 0-0 0, Drew Knutson 3-4 0-0 6, Billy Kegler 0-2 0-0 0, Joe Bemis 1-2 1-3 3. Totals 18-50 9-16 49.

UW-Stevens Point (65): Nick Bennett 6-10 2-3 14, Jason Kalsow 8-15 1-4 20, Eric Maus 3-5 1-2 7, Tamaris Relerford 0-2 0-0 0, Jon Krull 1-2 0-0 2, Brett Hirsch 0-3 0-0 0, Brad Kalsow 2-3 0-0 4, Steve Hicklin 0-2 3-4 3, Kyle Grusczynski 3-4 0-0 8, Cory Krautkramer 0-0 2-2 2, Brian Bauer 1-1 0-0 3, Mike Prey 1-2 0-0 2, Gbenga Awe 0-3 0-0. Totals 25-52 9-15 65.

UW-La Crosse	13	36	- 49
UW-Stevens Point	34	31	- 65

3-point goals: Stevens Point 6-13 (Relerford 0-2, Bennett 0-2, J. Kalsow 3-4, Hicklin 0-1, Grusczynski 2-3, Bauer 1-1), La Crosse 4-14 (Ask 0-3, Fehrenbach 3-6, Hall 1-3, Borchard 0-1, Huss 0-1). Total fouls: La Crosse 16, Stevens Point 10. Fouled out: none. Rebounds: Stevens Point 37 (Maus 11), La Crosse 29 (Werner 7). Turnovers: Stevens Point 12, La Crosse 10. Att.-1,814.

STEVENS POINT - The University of Wisconsin-Stevens Point men's basketball team didn't need much help building a lead early on against UW-La Crosse, as the Eagles lent them a helping hand with their icy touch in the first half.

The Eagles went 1 for 12 to start the contest, finished the half with just 13 points and could never pull themselves back as the Pointers rolled to a 65-49 Wisconsin Intercollegiate Athletic Conference victory at Quandt Fieldhouse.

"I felt we defended very well against this team tonight," UWSP coach Jack Bennett said. "We didn't give them a lot of easy stuff, and as a team we moved around very well. When your opponent only scores 13 points, you know things are working for you in that area."

While the Eagles struggled on the offensive end early on, the Pointers (12-1, 5-1 WIAC) chose to do the majority of their damage inside as they scored a dozen points in the paint while jumping out to a 20-8 lead in the first 13 minutes of play. Senior forward Jason Kalsow led the way, pouring in seven of his game-high 20 points during that run.

"We wanted to come out and set the tone defensively right away," Kalsow said. "La Crosse can be a very aggressive team, and we wanted to try and take that away from them and make some things happen for us on offense."

The Pointers continued to push their offensive plans in the second half as they connected on their first six shots and built a 23-point advantage. For the game, UWSP connected on 48 percent (25 of 52) of shots from the floor. Senior forward Nick Bennett added 14 points for the Pointers, but saw his streak of 35 straight games with a 3-pointer come to an end.

The Eagles (4-10, 1-4 WIAC), meanwhile, made only 18 of 50 shots (36 percent), and shot just 20 percent in the first half. Joe Werner paced UW-L with 12 points and seven rebounds.

"I think we were a little tentative," UW-L coach Ken Koelbl said. "We came in here a little bit in awe I think, and we were back on our heels. We need to do a better job of getting things going a little earlier in the game."

POINTERS
REACH OUT TO YOUNG FANS
Five children get to sit on bench with players

By Andrew Dowd

STEVENS POINT - A handful of kids got to sit on the same bench as the athletes they look up to at Saturday afternoon's University of Wisconsin-Stevens Point men's basketball game at Quandt Fieldhouse.

Aside from allowing children under 14 in to the game for free Saturday at the basketball team's Youth Day, five children won the chance to sit on the Pointer bench during the game.

In the team colors of purple and gold, Sarah Komasa, 12, a student at P.J. Jacobs Junior High School in Stevens Point, watched the game intently from her seat on the edge of the court.

A regular attendee of Pointers home games, Komasa hoped that sitting close to the players and getting closer to the game would give her some tips on how she can be a better basketball player at her school.

Though some children find the experience of sitting next to the basketball players intimidating because of their size, Tom Bertz, president of the University of Wisconsin-Stevens Point Men's Backcourt Club, said the kids usually enjoy their time on the bench.

"It's just a thrill for them to be able to do that," Bertz said.

During the game, the kids were on the edge of their seats, leaning forward to look down the court when the Pointers scored on UW-La Crosse.

Joe Beigel, 9, of Bancroft said he is a big fan of the Pointers, and he was all smiles when he sat down a few chairs from the team as the game began.

His favorite part of watching the game was seeing the Pointers sink three-point shots, but as for picking his favorite player, Beigel said, "I like all of 'em."

The Backcourt Club organizes Youth Day with the help of the university and the law firm of Anderson, O'Brien, Bertz, Skrenes and Golla to get children interested in basketball and create future Pointers fans.

This was the fourth year Youth Day had been held, and each year, Bertz said, the event grows larger and more children participate.

When the Pointers' lineup was announced at the beginning of the game, the five kids also were announced, and they ran through the two rows of players and stood on the court. At half-time, 20 basketballs signed by the team and coaches were given away to children in the audience, too.

DOUG WOJCIK

Top: Carlee Simon waits in anticipation to receive a basketball autographed by the Pointers team and coaches during halftime of the UWSP game. The promotion was sponsored by law firm Anderson, O'Brien, Bertz, Skrenes and Golla to help get children interested in basketaball and create future Pointers fan.

Below: Five lucky kids got to sit with the Pointers during their 65-49 win over UW-La Crosse.

DOUG WOJCIK

WISCONSIN
INTERCOLLEGIATE ATHLETIC CONFERENCE

Pointer men roll UW-Superior

By Scott Williams

SUPERIOR - The University of Wisconsin-Stevens Point men's basketball team held UW-Superior to 28 percent shooting from the field for a 77-42 victory Saturday in WIAC action.

Jason Kalsow scored 19 points, grabbed seven rebounds and had two blocked shots for the Pointers (13-1 overall, 6-1 WIAC). Nick Bennett added 17 points and three 3-pointers and Jon Krull finished with 13 points.

"It was really an outstanding defensive performance," UWSP coach Jack Bennett said. "We played great team defense and had only seven turnovers. They had great quickness and we were able to neutralize that. We played some man and a lot of zone."

UW-Superior defeated the Pointers last year.

"It was a big win because we lost to them last year," Bennett said. "It's a difficult road trip with weather colder than the North Pole. But we brought a lot of fire. We shot really well today."

POINTERS 77, SUPERIOR 42

UW-Stevens Point (77)--Relerford, Tamaris 1-2 4-4 6, Bennett, Nick 4-9 6-6 17, Krull, Jon 4-7 4-6 13, Kalsow, Jason 5-11 9-11 19, Maus, Eric 4-6 1-1 9, Lee, Shawn 1-1 0-0 2, Hirsch, Brett 2-3 0-0 4, Kalsow, Brad 0-0 0-0 0, Hicklin, Steve 0-1 0-0 0, Grusczynski, Kyle 0-1 0-0 0, Krautkramer, Cory 1-2 0-0 2, Bouche, Matt 0-0 0-0 0, Bauer, Brian 1-2 0-0 2, Prey, Mike 0-0 1-2 1, Awe, Gbenga 1-3 0-0 2

UW-Superior (42)--Reed, Laron 1-6 4-4 7, Rothschadl, Marc 2-11 0-0 4, McDonald, Amil 1-3 0-0 2, Turner, Kevin 0-3 0-0 0, Polkowski, Greg 1-1 0-0 2, Hillerbrandt, Tyler 0-0 0-0 0, Couto, Gus 2-5 0-0 5, Hebert, John 0-1 0-0 0, Bayiha Floyd Nyemeck 2-5 9-11 14, Collins, Courtney 0-0 0-0 0, Cobb, Leonard 3-8 2-2 8

UW-Stevens Point	42	35	77
UW-Superior	22	20	42

3-point goals: Stevens Point 4-11 (Bennett 3-5, J. Kalsow 0-1, Krull 1-2, Hicklin 0-1, Grusczynski 0-1, Krautkramer 0-1), Superior 3-21. Total fouls: Superior 23, Stevens Point 12. Fouled out: Superior-McDonald. Rebounds: Stevens Point 28 (Kalsow 7), Superior 32 (Cobb 11). Turnovers: Stevens Point 7, Superior 24.

FEATURE
TAMARIS RELERFORD

Pointer point guard brings football mentality

Top: Relerford has become more of a complete point guard, but can still fill it up when called upon to score.

Below: Relerford penetrates and looks for an open teammate.

By Scott Williams

Tamaris Relerford feels just as comfortable in shoulder pads and cleats as he does in shorts and basketball sneakers. A senior point guard on the University of Wisconsin-Stevens Point men's basketball team, Relerford had a number of Division I schools looking at him for football, including Minnesota.

Relerford brings that same hard-nosed, gritty, warrior mentality to the basketball court.

"We take our cue on defense from Tamaris out front. He will not back down from anyone and will throw his body in there," Pointer coach Jack Bennett said. "He's got that mentality whether he's going to the basket or making cuts to daylight."

There are nights when football pads would come in handy for Relerford. He picks up his share of floor burns diving for loose balls. And then there are the bumps and bruises he accumulates because of his fearless determination to fight through screens or take a charge.

At 5-foot-8 and a solid 176 pounds, however, Relerford felt for the sake of his well-being that basketball was the better sport to pursue in college.

"Football is just something I wanted to play because it made me tough for the basketball season," Relerford said. "Being around the game helped me out as far as being mentally and physically tough."

Speaking of tough, Relerford had a hard decision to make after his senior year at Beloit Memorial High School. A third-team all-state player, he passed on basketball offers from North Dakota State and Eastern Washington to play with the Pointers.

"I chose Stevens Point because I was aware of what the Bennetts had done there," Relerford said. "It was far enough away from home for me to get away. Yet, it was close enough for my family and friends to come watch me play."

Joining Relerford in Stevens Point was his best friend, Dwonne McAlister, who never felt comfortable at the school or with the basketball program. There were times when Relerford had his doubts if things would work out for him. He had thought that maybe he should have gone the Division I or II route.

"There were times when I was frustrated that I thought, 'I'm really not supposed to be here. I should be playing Division I,'" he said. "But I understood what it means to be a Pointer. It might have been a different story if we didn't win."

Part of his frustration came from spending his freshman season on the UW-Stevens Point campus red-shirting. But the real dilemma for Relerford came from dealing with the concept of being a scorer in high school to becoming a "true" point guard.

Coach Bennett insisted on that in order for his system to work. Relerford needed to be more concerned with distributing the ball and running the offense than how many points he scored.

"He could score, don't get me wrong, but that would hurt the offense we use. I'm very grateful to have a team made up of unselfish players, but especially a point guard that thinks unselfish," Bennett said.

"I think his greatest improvement has been his decision-making. When to push the ball and when to back off and run the half court offense. Tamaris has really become a player who has the ability to lead and make good decisions under pressure."

Not an easy adjustment for someone who averaged more than

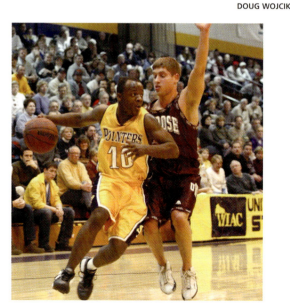

DOUG WOJCIK

Above: Senior point guard Tamaris Relerford.

PHOTO COURTESY OF UWSP SPORTS INFORMATION OFFICE

Bennett has seen his point guard grow just as much as a person, perhaps even more, than as a basketball player.

"Tamaris is a beautiful kid. He has a good sense of humor but is no-nonsense when he needs to be," the coach said. "I just felt there was a time when he was afraid to let people know he cared."

Relerford would counter that his coach had the wrong impression.

"He loves to yell at me about the length of my shorts and having to be cool," Relerford said. "But that is not what it's about."

Relerford eventually bought into Bennett's philosophy hook, line and sinker. He put his red-shirt season to good use, serving as an understudy to then point guard Brent Larson and learned how to handle the duties of the position in the Pointer system.

"I learned a lot from Brent," Relerford said. "When you think about a point guard here you don't have to score. You have to do the little things or you're not doing the job. I would much rather make an assist that leads to a 3-point play now."

Relerford took over the point job from Neal Krajnik midway through his junior season. Not that Relerford isn't capable of hurting teams with his shot, despite never averaging more than 5 points during any of his four seasons. In fact, none other than senior Pointer sharp-shooter Nick Bennett feels Relerford is one of the best shooters on the team.

"He's a great shooter. When teams concentrate on Jason (Kalsow) or me, he's going to make them pay," Nick Bennett said. "He's evolved into an exciting college point guard who is willing to sacrifice his own shots to get the ball to other players."

There have been more than a handful of games this season when Relerford has delivered the dagger with a big 3-point shot. Just ask UW-Whitewater.

The Warhawks discovered just how lethal he can be last Saturday when Relerford drained a pair of long-range shots during a decisive run in the second half that helped propel UWSP to the Wisconsin Intercollegiate Athletic Conference Tournament championship.

And it's the resounding cheers he heard from the crowd at the Quandt Fieldhouse after hitting those bombs that makes Relerford happy he became a Pointer.

"I'll always remember playing in this gymnasium. The atmosphere in buildings around the conference is nothing like in here," Relerford said. "I wouldn't want to be anything but a Pointer."

20 points a game in high school.

And his comfort level wasn't necessarily limited to the basketball court. Relerford grew up in more of an urban setting and had very little experience in a predominantly rural environment. He said the transition was easier than might be expected.

"Beloit was a really diverse city. I've always been someone who is open to new things and looks forward to meeting new people," Relerford said.

WISCONSIN
INTERCOLLEGIATE ATHLETIC CONFERENCE

TOP-RANKED POINTERS KNOCK OUT TITANS
Zone defense by UWSP roughs up UW-Oshkosh

By Scott Williams

The University of Wisconsin-Oshkosh had the top-ranked and defending Division III national champion men's basketball team on the ropes Tuesday night.

UW-Stevens Point took one body shot after another before landing a haymaker in the form of a 3-2 zone. UWSP outscored the Titans 24-5 over the final 10:12 of the first half, and the Pointers went on to knock out the Titans 69-44 before 1,159 at Quandt Fieldhouse.

"This was like a boxing match. You measure your opponent and take some early shots," UWSP coach Jack Bennett said. "You look to find some openings and get tougher and tougher in the middle rounds."

The scorecard had Oshkosh with the early lead on points - 18-7 to be exact. However, before the referees could call it, Bennett switched to the zone defense. Shooting over a zone is one thing. Shooting over one of the tallest zones in the Wisconsin Intercollegiate Athletic Conference, with no player shorter than 6-foot-4, was downright maddening.

"It's a sliding 3-2 and has some matchup (zone) principles. In the end all I know is that it bothers teams," Bennett said.

What started out so promising for the Titans - ranked No. 25 in the latest D3hoops.com poll - quickly turned into a nightmare. After hitting seven of its first 14 shots from the field, Oshkosh (12-5, 5-3 WIAC) connected on just two of its final 10 attempts from the floor.

"We gave them a good shot at the beginning and they didn't flinch," Oshkosh coach Ted Van Dellen said. "We did exactly what we wanted. That was take the ball right at them.

"But he (coach Bennett) did the smart thing. He went fishing for something that would work and found the right lure I guess."

Kerry Gibson, the Titans 7-foot-1 sophomore center took care of business in the paint. The Pointers struggled against Gibson's size. He scored six quick points and finished with a team-high 18, including a trio of dunks.

"We were concentrating on getting the ball in the post. When you don't have an outside game to complement they were able to pack it in," said Van Dellen. "When Kerry turned with the ball he had three guys on him. He couldn't go right or left."

The Pointers (14-1, 7-1 WIAC) were willing to let Gibson get his points. Of more importance was making sure the Titans' Jim Capelle and Andy Jahnke never got untracked on the perimeter. Mission accomplished as the Oshkosh tandem went a combined 5-for-20 from the field.

"I don't know if we caught them on a bad night shooting or what," said Pointer senior

Top: Senior Jason Kalsow drives past Oshkosh center Kerry Gibson.

Below: Jason Kalsow steps outside for a three-pointer in UWSP's 69-44 win.

DOUG WOJCIK

DOUG WOJCIK

POINTERS 69, TITANS 44

UW-OSHKOSH (44) - Jim Capelle 3-11 2-4 8, Kerry Gibson 6-9 6-9 18, Andy Fernholz 3-6 2-3 9, Chad Doedens 1-2 0-0 2, Andy Jahnke 2-9 0-0 5, Lallensack 0-1 0-0 0, Kyle Johnson 1-6 0-0 2, Nathan Wesener 0-0 0-2 0, Peter Warning 0-2 0-0 0. Totals 16-46 10-18 44.

UW-STEVENS POINT (69) - Nick Bennett 7-15 4-4 21, Jason Kalsow 8-16 5-5 22, Eric Maus 2-5 1-1 5, Tamaris Relerford 0-1 0-0 0, Jon Krull 3-6 4-4 10, Kyle Grusczynski 3-5 0-0 9, Matt Bouche 0-1 2-2 2. Totals 23-49 16-16 69.

UW-Oshkosh	23	21	- 44
UW-Stevens Point	31	38	- 69

3-point goals: Oshkosh 2-16 (Capelle 0-5, Fernholz 1-2, Jahnke 1-5, Lallensack 0-1, Johnson 0-3), Stevens Point 7-15 (Bennett 3-5, J. Kalsow 1-4, Relerford 0-1, Grusczynski 3-5). Total fouls: Oshkosh 18, Stevens Point 17. Fouled out: none. Rebounds: Oshkosh 27 (Gibson 6), Stevens Point 35 (Bennett 9). Turnovers: Oshkosh 12, Stevens Point 10. Assists: Oshkosh 6, Stevens Point 11. Att. - 1,159.

Kyle Grusczynski who at 6-foot-6 was the long arm of the law in the zone and drained 3 of 5 treys from downtown coming off the bench.

"We knew in order to get back in the game we had to buckle up on defense. We were flying around and challenging as many shots as we could."

Ironically, just when the Titans started to cool off, Nick Bennett and the Pointers began to heat up. Bennett, one of five seniors, scored 12 of his 21 points in the final 9:54 of the first half as the Pointers made eight out of their last 13 shots.

A 14-0 spurt during that time helped UWSP turn an 11-point deficit into a 31-23 lead at halftime. Jason Kalsow made Gibson play defense on the other end of the court and finished with a game-high 22 points.

"They have four seniors starting and another coming off the bench. They been through this," Van Dellen said. "Our guys are still searching on how to get there."

The Titans made an early charge in the second half, using a 7-0 run to close the gap to 39-36 with 14:24 remaining. After a timeout, Jon Krull led the Pointers on an 18-1 run that blew the game open. Krull scored eight of his 10 points after intermission. During the UWSP charge, the Titans went face-to-face with the zone again. The result was an 11:47 stretch in which Oshkosh failed to make a field goal.

Game over.

"We're communicating better in our zone. We make it tough to get good looks, and tonight we were quick enough to get to the perimeter shooters," Kalsow said.

Left: Tamaris Relerford drives to the hoop for a finger roll.

Center: Nick Bennett looks to score. Bennett finished with 21 points.

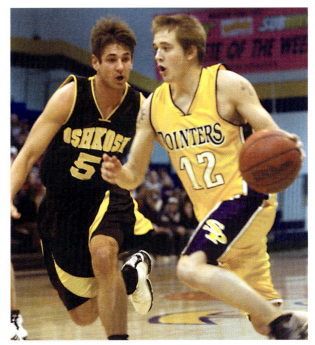

Right: Shawn Lee drives past UW-Oshkosh guard Chad Doedens.

DOUG WOJCIK

THE SEASON
NONCONFERENCE

Pointers men's basketball comes up big with bench player

Left: Brian Bauer hit all five of his shots from the field in the Pointers 79-49 victory over Edgewood.

TOM CHARLESWORTH

By Scott Williams

The University of Wisconsin-Stevens Point men's basketball team had nothing to worry about on the scoreboard Thursday night.

That is not to say there weren't some anxious moments. Jason Kalsow picked up a pair of quick fouls. Point guard Tamaris Relerford went down with a foot injury. No need to panic. Brian Bauer came to the rescue.

The Auburndale native came off the bench to score 10 points, hitting all five shots from the field, as the top-ranked Pointers rolled over Edgewood College 79-49 at the Quandt Fieldhouse.

The powerfully built power forward even did his best point guard impersonation. After a steal, Bauer demonstrated deft ball-handling skills as he dribbled the length of the court for a lay-up.

"I don't think so," said Bauer of his aspirations to take over some minutes in the backcourt if Relerford is forced to miss a period of time. "When your number gets called, you need to come in and show you can provide a spark off the bench. Tonight the basket looked huge to me."

UWSP (15-1) owns the top scoring defense in NCAA Division III and Edgewood found out why as they became the fourth straight opponent to be held under 50 points. There was a time when the Eagles, who became UWSP's 43rd straight non-conference victim, might have been happy to score 40 after missing their first 13 field goal attempts.

Seth Cooper ended the drought with 7:55 left in the opening half when he found the target from 3-point range. That brought Edgewood within 18-7. All Pointer coach Jack Bennett could think about was the three consecutive 3-pointers the Eagles (10-7) drained midway through the second half.

"In my mind, all I could think about was is this good enough to beat a La Crosse or Platteville," Bennett said. "I want to keep them hungry on the defensive end. I thought we went through the motions for a period in the second half."

Cooper was the only Eagle who decided to make the trip from Madison. The Eagles' leading scorer at 19.1 points per game, Cooper was the lone Edgewood player to find his way into double digits with a game-high 22 points. He was helped by an 11 for 14 effort at the free throw line. But Cooper didn't get much help. Edgewood shot 13 percent (2 of 16) in the first half and he accounted for both baskets.

"I think at times there can be an intimidation factor because of how we play," said Bennett.

There were no such shooting problems for the Pointers, who shot a sizzling 61.4 percent for the game. Part of the reason was the unselfish manner in which UWSP ran its offense. What may have been an open look was bypassed for an even better shot. The result was the Pointers had 12 assists on their 16 first-half baskets. For the game, 20 passes led directly to hoops. The biggest beneficiaries were Nick Bennett and Kalsow, who shared scoring honors with 16 points apiece.

"That's unbelievable in today's age of basketball with so much one-on-one and individual stuff," coach Bennett said. "When a team tries to be unselfish, it translates into that kind of play. If we don't play team ball, we're not as effective."

POINTERS 79, EAGLES 49

EDGEWOOD COLLEGE (49) - Charlie Averkamp 0-6 2-2 2, Seth Cooper 5-11 11-14 22, Greg Blaska 2-6 3-4 7, Justin Kuhnau 0-3 0-0 0, David Michalkiewicz 2-6 1-2 6, Tyler O'Brien 0-3 0-0 0, Kyle Scott 0-1 0-0 0, Nick Lehman 1-3 0-0 3, John Fahey 2-4 1-3 7, Luke Wainwright 0-1 2-2 2. Totals 12-44 20-27 49.

UW-STEVENS POINT (79) - Nick Bennett 5-11 3-3 16, Jason Kalsow 8-10 0-0 16, Eric Maus 4-7 0-0 8, Tamaris Relerford 0-2 0-0 0, Jon Krull 4-5 0-0 8, Shawn Lee 0-1 0-0 0, Brett Hirsch 1-2 0-1 2, Brad Kalsow 1-2 0-0 2, Kyle Grusczynski 2-5 0-0 5, Matt Bouche 2-3 0-0 4, Brian Bauer 5-5 0-0 10, Mike Prey 1-1 1-1 3, Gbenga Awe 2-3 1-3 5. Totals 35-57 5-8 79.

Edgewood	19	30	- 49
UW-Stevens Point	37	42	- 79

3-point goals: Edgewood 5-16 (Averkamp 0-2, Cooper 1-2, Kuhnau 0-3, Michalkiewicz 1-2, Scott 0-1, Lehman 1-2, Fahey 2-4), Stevens Point 4-16 (Bennett 3-7, J. Kalsow 0-2, Relerford 0-2, B. Kalsow 0-1, Grusczynski 1-4). Total fouls: Edgewood 12, Stevens Point 17. Fouled out: none. Technical foul: Edgewood bench. Rebounds: Edgewood 27 (Cooper 6), Stevens Point 34 (J. Kalsow 8). Turnovers: Edgewood 14, Stevens Point 9.

Left: Jon Krull and Nick Bennett battle for an offensive rebound against UW-La Crosse.

DOUG WOJCIK

WISCONSIN
INTERCOLLEGIATE ATHLETIC CONFERENCE

Pointers survive UW-LaCrosse in overtime win

By Scott Williams

POINTERS 63, UW-LA CROSSE 62

UW-Stevens Point(63)--Grusczynski, Kyle 0-3 0-0 0, Bennett, Nick 8-16 4-4 23, Krull, Jon 2-7 0-2 4, Kalsow, Jason 7-13 3-4 22, Maus, Eric 3-4 5-6 11, Relerford, Tamaris 0-1 0-0 0, Lee, Shawn 0-1 0-0 0, Kalsow, Brad 0-1 0-0 0, Bauer, Brian 1-1 0-0 3

UW-La Crosse(62)--Fehrenbach, Chris 7-16 0-0 20, Hall, Josh 3-6 1-1 9, Ask, Chris 3-12 4-6 10, Werner, Joe 2-6 0-0 4, Owen, Timothy 4-10 2-2 12, Conigliaro, Marcus 1-3 0-0 3, Kegler, Billy 0-0 0-0 0, Bemis, Joe 1-2 2-2 4

UW-Stevens Point	29	26	8	- 63
UW-La Crosse	30	25	7	- 62

3-point goals: Stevens Point 9-21 (Bennett 3-7, J. Kalsow 5-8, Relerford 0-1, Grusczynski 0-3, Bauer 1-1, Lee 0-1). Total fouls: La Crosse 16, Stevens Point 13. Fouled out: La Crosse-Fehrenbach. Rebounds: La Crosse 34 (Werner 11), Stevens Point 29 (Kalsow 8). Turnovers: La Crosse 11, Stevens Point 12. Assists: La Crosse 13, Stevens Point 14.

Having hit numerous big shots over the past four years, Jason Kalsow and Nick Bennett delivered again for the UW-Stevens Point men's basketball team.

The senior duo both knocked down three-pointers in the final minute of overtime to rally the Pointers from a five-point deficit and pull out a heartstopping 63-62 victory at UW-La Crosse on Saturday at Mitchell Hall.

Bennett drained a three-pointer with one-minute left and, after an Eagles' turnover with 25 seconds left, the Pointers found Kalsow in the right corner for a game-winning three-pointer with six seconds left. Both players played all 45 minutes in the hard-fought contest. UW-La Crosse had a shot fall short at the buzzer as the nation's top-ranked Division III team hung on for the win. UW-Stevens Point is now 16-1 overall and 8-1 in the Wisconsin Intercollegiate Athletic Conference, while UW-La Crosse fell to 5-13 overall and 2-7 in the league.

Both teams hit big shots throughout the game as UW-Stevens Point's Eric Maus drained a pair of clutch free throws with 30 seconds left in regulation to give the Pointers a 55-52 lead. UW-La Crosse tied the game when Josh Hall drove the baseline and was fouled, throwing up a shot that bounced high off the backboard and in before sinking the tying free throw with six seconds left. Kalsow missed a three-pointer at the other end, but Bennett had a successful rebound put-back at the buzzer that was ruled late and the game went to overtime.

In overtime, Hall hit a three-pointer to give the Eagles a 60-57 lead with 2:15 left and Chris Ask drained a jumper that put UW-La Crosse ahead 62-57 with 1:19 left before Bennett and Kalsow's heroics.

UW-La Crosse opened up a nine-point lead in the first half on the strength of six first half three-pointers. However, the Pointers crawled to within one at 30-29 at halftime. UW-Stevens Point had a 9-0 run in the second half to build a 40-34 advantage with 13:54 remaining, but the Eagles hung tough, scoring seven straight points as Chris Fehrenbach hit back-to-back three-pointers for a 41-40 lead.

Bennett answered with a three-pointer and a three-point play for a 46-41 UW-Stevens Point lead with 7:44 left, but UW-La Crosse hung within five points as Fehrenbach hit three-pointers with 4:45 left and 2:05 remaining to pull the Eagles within 53-52.

Kalsow finished with a career-high five three-pointers and totaled 22 points, eight rebounds and eight assists. Bennett led all scorers with 23 points and Fehrenbach had six three-pointers and 20 points for the Eagles, who had 16 offensive rebounds

FEATURE
NICK BENNETT

Latest Bennett basketball star thrives with hard work ethic

Top: UWSP senior All-American Nick Bennett.

Below: Nick Bennett has expanded his offensive game over the past two years allowing him to drive past defenders who play him solely as a three-point shooter.

By Scott Williams

Common sense suggests that when University of Wisconsin-Stevens Point senior forward Nick Bennett entered the world he was born to be a basketball player.

His father, Jack Bennett, was a high school coach at Wisconsin Rapids Lincoln and Rhinelander before taking over the helm at UWSP. His uncle, Dick Bennett, had stops at UWSP, UW-Green Bay and the University of Wisconsin on his coaching resume. Nick's cousin Tony Bennett played at UWGB and had a cup of coffee with Charlotte in the NBA.

Heck, with a gene pool like that forensic scientists would be hard-pressed to reach any conclusion other than Nick Bennett had basketball star written all over his DNA.

Not so fast.

"I admit I had my doubts. There was a time I wondered if I would ever play here," Nick Bennett said. "I was never a great high school player. I was just taller than most players. I thought maybe I could be a role player."

Bennett, who measures in at 6-foot-6, has developed into much more than a role player. He is a self-made basketball star at the Division III level.

"I talk about how I feel Jason (Kalsow) is one of the most complete players at our level, and deserves to be considered for player of the year. Nick isn't far off," UWSP coach Jack Bennett said.

Countless hours spent in the gym shooting thousands of jump shots. Day after day in the weight room to try to add some bulk to his lanky frame.

Those reasons are why Nick Bennett is a returning first team All-Wisconsin Intercollegiate Athletic Conference selection, and poised to finish his career ranked among the top 10 in scoring in school history. He currently is 10th on the all-time list with 1,386 points.

It has absolutely nothing to do with his family tree.

"I would have been surprised if I hadn't seen the determination, work ethic and love for the game he demonstrated in the off-season," Pointer assistant coach Bob Semling said. "Nick capitalized on every area he needed to work on. Part of it was the natural progression of maturity."

When Bennett showed up for practice after a solid prep career at Stevens Point Area Senior High, a number of Pointer players were doing double-takes and wondering if he was in the right place. Here was this gangly kid whose jump shot had little if any rotation. What Bennett lacked in quickness he failed to make up for with his vertical jump.

"I was like, 'Who is this little stiff kid?'" Pointer senior point guard Tamaris Relerford said. "He moves so different that any player who guards him after he scores are like, 'How and why?'"

"Nick is real skilled fundamentally. He has developed a sense that every time he shoots the ball it's going to go in. When I pass him the ball, I expect the shot to go in."

Nick Bennett was redshirted that first year. A move he admits was the best thing that could have happened to him. No one realized Bennett wasn't ready physically or mentally for the nightly pounding in the WIAC more than himself. So it was off to the weight room to gain some much-needed strength.

"It was definitely very important for me to mature physically and get use to the speed of the college game. I've put on 25 pounds of muscle since my first year here," said Bennett of his redshirt year. "I would've had trouble getting my shot off or getting off screens without adding some strength."

After averaging 5.6 points a game as a freshman, Bennett contributed 13.5 points a contest the next season.

PHOTO COURTESY OF UWSP SPORTS INFORMATION OFFICE

TOM CHARLESWORTH

TOM CHARLESWORTH

Above: Nick Bennett finished his career as the number three all-time scorer at UWSP with 1,646 points.

While his shot may look unorthodox - some major league pitchers would envy such a knuckleball - Nick Bennett has always been a serious shooting threat. He shot 60 percent from the field, including 52 percent from 3-point range, as a sophomore.

That was only a preview of what was to come. Semling saw a major transformation in Nick's game take place around the midpoint of his junior season.

"I would say he was just a shooter as a sophomore. But he really expanded his game at that point. He would make people pay if they extended out on him either with a pass or off the dribble," Semling said. "Now you can't say he is just a shooter."

Nick Bennett proceeded to put together one of the most magnificent stretches of shooting anyone had seen at the Division III level, or any level. He entered the so-called "zone" where there wasn't a defense - zone, man-to-man or gimmick - that could slow Bennett down, let alone stop him.

Bennett's numbers during the Pointers' national championship run were mind-blowing: He averaged 25.5 points a game in the tournament and shot a sizzling 60 percent (21 for 35) from behind the arc.

All the numbers were nice, but what really impressed coach Jack Bennett was Nick's penchant for coming through in clutch situations. Jack can think of at least four occasions when Nick drained a big shot in a key situation over the past two years.

"Nick may be the greatest pressure player I've coached. I just scratch my head over the number of pressure big shots I've seen go in for him," Jack Bennett said. "There are no guarantees you're going to make those shots. But I think you have to be willing to risk that and put yourself in that position."

If there were any doubts, the skinny kid with the ugly shot had officially arrived on the Division III basketball scene.

The kid Houston Rockets scout Brett Johnson called "maybe the best non-athletic basketball player I've ever seen," after an exhibition game with Marquette earlier this season, was named the most valuable player in the Division III Final Four.

Bennett concluded the season averaging 17.2 points a game - identical to the average that he is putting up each game this season.

Perhaps no one has benefited more from his outside shooting touch than Pointer senior forward Jason Kalsow, who is 39 points shy of breaking the school's all-time career scoring record.

"His outside shooting makes it so much easier on me on the inside. Even more so when he's on my side, then it's like pick your poison," Kalsow said. "From what I've seen, he's become a more complete player."

Bennett has been able to enjoy the wild ride alongside his father. The father-son and coach-player relationship has been everything Jack Bennett could ask for, and more. Admittedly tougher on Nick than other players at times, Jack is thankful he got the chance to coach Nick, and win a national title in the process.

"Imagine Brett Favre winning the Super Bowl and his dad being the coach as close as they were. Or Michael Jordan having his father on the bench when he won all those NBA titles," Jack Bennett said. "I feel doubly-blessed. Not only as a parent, but to be his coach and win our first national championship."

Unlike his older brother Jay, Nick Bennett never had a chance to be coached by his father at the youth or high school levels. When the opportunity presented itself with the Pointers, Nick couldn't have imagined playing for anyone else. Even though he knew it wouldn't be a walk on the basketball court.

"Anytime I feel bad for myself, I feel worse for my brother who had him as a coach for eight years," Nick joked. "I wouldn't trade this experience for anything. I love him as my coach, and that he's my dad makes it more special."

Another WIAC regular season title - the fifth in six seasons - and Division III national championship would be the perfect ending.

WISCONSIN
INTERCOLLEGIATE ATHLETIC CONFERENCE

Pointers fall to Platteville

By Scott Williams

Right: The Pointers attempt to slow down the high scoring Pioneers.

PHOTO COURTESY OF ANDY McNEIL

PLATTEVILLE - Forget any thoughts of back-to-back NCAA Division III national titles for now. The University of Wisconsin-Stevens Point men's basketball team has a fight on its hands to win the Wisconsin Intercollegiate Athletic Conference regular-season title.

UWSP fell out of sole possession of first place in the WIAC after suffering a 73-58 setback at the hands of UW-Platteville at Williams Fieldhouse on Wednesday night.

The top-ranked Pointers (16-2) and Platteville, no strangers to WIAC championships, now share the top spot in the conference at 8-2.

"This thing is far from over," UWSP coach Jack Bennett said. "One way or another, we're going to be in the hunt until the end."

Defense - a key ingredient in the Pointers' success this season - was made to look ordinary by the Pioneers, and Brad Reitzner in particular. Reitzner blistered the nets for career-high matching 31 points, with much of his damage coming from behind the 3-point arc.

The shooting guard had his radar honed in all night long, connecting on five of his nine attempts from 3-point land. Reitzner finished 9 for 15 from the field. In his nine previous games against the Pointers, Reitzner had averaged 8.8 points a game.

"He's (Reitzner) been struggling, but he's too good a player to struggle. After he hit a couple with the shot clock winding down you could tell he was feeling it," Bennett said.

"Perhaps we should have doubled him. He's just a good player. An All-American caliber player."

Reitzner wasn't the only Pioneer with a hot hand. Brandon Temperly chipped in with 13 points and Mark Gossens added 10. Platteville (13-5) wound up shooting 67 percent (26 for 39) for the game. Opponents came into Wednesday shooting only 35 percent from the field against the Pointers.

Despite the Pioneers' hot hand, UWSP hung tough in the opening half and only trailed 30-29 at intermission. A slow start to the second half doomed the Pointers, who were outscored 13-2 over the first 5:44 of the half to extend the deficit to 43-31.

"I think the thing I'm most disappointed about is our start in the second half. We came out on our heels and they took it to us," Bennett said.

Another problem was finding a player or three to complement the 1-2 punch of Nick Bennett and Jason Kalsow, who each scored 17 points. The next best scoring output was eight by Eric Maus.

"This is a team-oriented offense. If we don't get a little more from some other players, then we lean on them (Nick Bennett and Kalsow) too much," coach Bennett said.

POINTERS 58, PIONEERS 73

UW-STEVENS POINT (58) - Tamaris Relerford 2-7 0-0 6, Nick Bennett 6-12 2-2 17, Jon Krull 1-2 0-0 2, Jason Kalsow 5-10 6-6 17, Eric Maus 2-2 4-6 8, Shawn Lee 1-1 0-0 3, Brad Kalsow 0-2 0-0 0, Kyle Grusczynski 0-2 0-0 0, Brian Bauer 2-4 0-0 5. Totals 19-42 8-21 58.

UW-PLATTEVILLE (73) - Brad Reitzner 9-15 8-9 31, Sean Krause 3-3 0-1 6, Brandon Temperly 4-7 4-8 13, Mark Gossens 4-5 2-3 10, Jeff Skemp 2-2 1-1 5, LaVon Crawford 4-7 0-2 8. Totals 26-39 15-24 73.

UW-Stevens Point	29	29	- 58
UW-Platteville	30	43	- 73

3-point goals: Stevens Point 8-21 (Relerford 2-5, Bennett 3-7, J. Kalsow 1-2, Lee 1-1, B. Kalsow 0-2, Grusczynski 0-2, Bauer 1-2). Total fouls: Stevens Point 18, Platteville 14. Fouled out: none. Rebounds: Stevens Point 17 (J. Kalsow 6), Platteville 24 (Crawford 7). Turnovers: Stevens Point 12, Platteville 16.

WISCONSIN
INTERCOLLEGIATE ATHLETIC CONFERENCE

Left: Eric Maus blocks the shot.

PHOTOS COURTESY OF LAYNE PITT AND UW-STOUT SPORTS INFORMATION

UWSP beats Stout, still in first in WIAC

By Scott Williams

MENOMONIE - The University of Wisconsin-Stevens Point men's basketball team's 64-52 win over UW-Stout on Saturday was about as big as it has been for the Pointers so far this season.

The win moves UWSP (17-2, 9-2 WIAC) into a half-game lead in the race for the conference title as UW-Platteville was idle on Saturday. Pointers coach Jack Bennett said Saturday's tussle with the Blue Devils was reminiscent of their NCAA Division III national championship run last year.

"We got huge performances out of (Nick) Bennett and (Jason) Kalsow but also some solid play off the bench. It really was a team performance and that's the only way you're going to beat a team as athletic and strong as Stout," Bennett said.

The Pointers came out of the first half down 33-31, but exploded in the second half with a 33-19 advantage. Part of the Pointers' success came at the expense of Stout's deteriorating offense. After hitting 42.9 percent (12 for 28) from the floor in the first half, the Blue Devils were just 26.7 percent (8 for 30) in the second half. UWSP maintained an even 50 percent (12 for 24) in each half.

The Pointers' main scoring tandem - Bennett and Kalsow - were back at it again as Bennett put up a team-high 27 points and Kalsow added 21. Eric Maus hauled in 11 rebounds for the Pointers - all on the defensive end of the ball.

Coach Bennett said he isn't going to let the win get inside the heads of his players as the season still trudges on. The Pointers begin a series of four home games next Saturday beginning with UW-Eau Claire.

"The win doesn't guarantee anything but I can't think of a better way to come back and play at home than this game on the road," Bennett said.

POINTERS 64, BLUE DEVILS 52

UW-Stevens Point (64): Tamaris Relerford 0-2 0-0 0 0, Nick Bennett 11-17 3-4 27, Jon Krull 0-2 0-0 0, Jason Kalsow 7-12 5-6 21, Eric Maus 3-6 1-2 8, Kyle Grusczynski 2-6 0-2 5, Brian Bauer 1-3 1-3 3. Totals: 24-48 10-17 64.

UW-Stout (52): Adam Chandler 6-12 0-0 16, Greg Chaissoon 3-8 0-2 6, Ryan Stangl 3-13 2-2 10, Terry Farmer 1-4 0-0 2, Jacob Nonemacher 1-4 1-2 3, Jesse Huser 1-2 0-0 2, Kailus Coleman 3-8 0-0 8, Luke Loney 0-2 0-0 0, Eric Heisler 1-3 1-2 3. Totals: 20-58 4-10 52.

UW-Stevens Point	31	33	- 64
UW-Stout	33	19	- 52

3-pointers - UWSP: 6-13 (Relerford 0-2, Bennett 2-5, Kalsow 2-3, Maus 1-1, Grusczynski 1-2); Stout: 8-22 (Chandler 4-8, Stangl 2-8, Huser 0-1, Coleman 2-3, Loney 0-2). **Rebounds -** UWSP: 34 (Maus 11); Stout: 35 (Nonemacher 7). **Assists -** UWSP: 11 (Relerford, Kalsow 4); Stout: 8 (Stangl 2). **Steals -** UWSP: 3 (Relerford 2); Stout: 7 (Chandler 2). **Personal Fouls -** UWSP: 15; Stout 14.

WISCONSIN
INTERCOLLEGIATE ATHLETIC CONFERENCE

Defending champs roll past Eau Claire

Right: Gbenga Awe goes up high to block the shot of UW-Eau Claire player Dan Archambault.

DOUG WOJCIK

By Scott Williams

Jason Kalsow entered Saturday night's game 39 points shy of tying the all-time career scoring record at the University of Wisconsin-Stevens Point.

He nearly set the new mark in one night. Perhaps the only thing that kept him from rewriting the record book was writer's cramp.

UW-Eau Claire could not stop Kalsow, who scored a career-high 31 points as the Pointers blew out the Blugolds 83-55 at the Quandt Fieldhouse. In the process, UWSP maintained a share of the Wisconsin Intercollegiate Athletic Conference lead with Platteville at 10-2.

"The record is not my main focus out there. That will come through the team system we run," Kalsow said.

The senior from Huntley (Ill.) showed all the variety in his game. Kalsow scored off lay-ups on cuts to the basket. Then, there was an array of pull up jumpers. However, the real damage came from behind the 3-point line where Kalsow showed his range by connecting on 3 of 5 attempts.

The coup de grace came in the form of a couple thunderous dunks. Kalsow scored 16 of his points in the opening half enabling UWSP to open up a 40-27 lead. He finished 11 for 15 from the field.

Even Blugolds coach Terry Gibbons sat back on the bench and enjoyed the performance turned in by Kalsow.

"Kalsow is just a man. In my 25 years of college coaching, I've never seen a performance like that one," Gibbons said. "I was in amazement. I couldn't help but smile from my seat."

One reason why Kalsow and the rest of the Pointers were free to do some serious damage was because the Blugolds turned all their attention on Nick Bennett. After a 71-50 loss at the hands of UWSP in the first meeting, Gibbons felt a need to try something different.

"My philosophy was I would rather try something different and fail, than fail and not try anything at all," Gibbons explained.

This was one experiment that was destined for failure. What looked like box-and-one turned out to be more like a Swiss cheese defense. While Bennett contributed a quiet 12 points, the gimmick defense left plenty of holes on the perimeter for UWSP. As a team, the Pointers shot a red-hot 54 percent (13 of 24) from behind the arc.

"When we take shots in a rhythm off a good pass and not forcing shots as the shot clock is winding down, we're going to shoot well," UWSP coach Jack Bennett said. "We took 3s in the context of our offense. When we do that we're pretty deadly from the outside."

And there were many volunteers on the Pointers to take advantage of all the openings. At the top of the list was Tamaris Relerford, who finished with 12 points on 4 for 6 shooting from 3-point land.

Steve Hicklin liked the defense as he drained a pair of 3-pointers while Jon Krull preferred to do his scoring around the basket as a result of offensive rebounds and cuts to the hoop. He contributed eight points.

The results was 22 assists on 29 baskets.

"Those are the kind of games you pray for. We got our role players to step up tonight," coach Bennett said. "In the second half, I thought we delivered the haymaker on both ends of the court."

POINTERS 83, BLUGOLDS 55

UW-EAU CLAIRE (55) - Kale Proksch 1-2 0-2 2, Will Jefferson 2-7 2-2 6, Buck Smith 3-5 4-4 10, Casey Drake 6-12 3-5 15, Dan Archambault 5-15 8-9 19, Zack Ryan 0-1 0-0 0, Jesse Breidenbach 0-0 0-1 0, Colin Walsh 0-2 0-0 0, Matt Riley 0-1 0-0 0, Jared Bardon 1-4 0-0 3, Chad Honl 0-2 0-0 0. Totals 18-51 17-23 55.

UW-STEVENS POINT (83) - Jon Krull 4-9 0-2 8, Jason Kalsow 11-15 6-8 31, Eric Maus 1-2 0-0 2, Tamaris Relerford 4-8 0-0 12, Nick Bennett 3-4 3-4 12, Brett Hirsch 1-1 0-2 2, Brad Kalsow 0-3 1-2 1, Steve Hicklin 2-3 0-0 6, Kyle Grusczynski 1-3 0-0 3, Cory Krautkramer 0-3 0-0 0, Brian Bauer 1-3 0-0 2, Mike Prey 1-1 0-0 2, Tyler Doyle 0-0 2-2 2. Totals 29-55 12-20 83.

UW-Eau Claire	27	28	- 55
UW-Stevens Point	40	43	- 83

3-point goals: Eau Claire 2-16 (Jefferson 0-4, Drake 0-1, Archambault 1-5, Riley 0-1, Bardon 1-3 Honl 0-2), Stevens Point 13-24 (Krull 0-1, J. Kalsow 3-5, Relerford 4-6, Bennett 3-4, B. Kalsow 0-2, Hicklin 2-3, Grusczynski 1-2, Bauer 0-1). Total fouls: Eau Claire 17, Stevens Point 16. Fouled out: none. Rebounds: Eau Claire 32 (Drake 6), Stevens Point 32 (Krull, J. Kalsow 5). Att. - 2,370.

FEATURE
JASON KALSOW

Kalsow keeps climbing

By Scott Williams

Top: Kalsow is highly-regarded for his passing ability.

Below: Jason Kalsow leads the break against Marquette. Kalsow has remarkable ball-handling skills for a player his size.

DOUG WOJCIK

UWSP SPORTS INFORMATION OFFICE

Jason Kalsow probably won't send University of Wisconsin-Stevens Point basketball fans flying out of their seats with a thunderous, backboard-breaking dunk.

He probably doesn't have the God-given natural athletic ability of former Pointer and NBA standout Terry Porter.

Tim Naegeli, the Pointers' all-time leading scorer, probably was a better pure shooter. Former Pointers Josh Iserloth, Jon Julius and Brant Bailey were arguably more of a load in the post. But when it's all said and done, no Pointer will be able to boast a more productive and successful career than Kalsow.

"Jason is one of the most complete players in all of college basketball. He is definitely the most complete player at the Division III level," UWSP coach Jack Bennett said.

All of the players listed above may soon be looking up at Kalsow on the scoring list. Barring any serious health issues, the 6-foot-7 senior center is on pace to break the school's all-time career scoring record.

Kalsow enters tonight's huge Wisconsin Intercollegiate Athletic Conference road game at UW-Whitewater seventh on the scoring list with 1,434 points. He needs 216 points-- an average of 13.5 points--over the final 16 games of the regular season to surpass Naegeli. Kalsow is averaging 18.6 points a game this year.

"Just to have my name be mentioned with them is a huge accomplishment. It's something never in my wildest dreams I would have imagined," Kalsow said. "It's something in a couple years that will be really special."

What Kalsow possesses is a basketball IQ second to none, and better athletic ability than he is given credit for. And if that is not enough, Kalsow is driven by a competitive internal inferno to succeed on the court.

He is just as comfortable stepping behind the 3-point arc to swish a jumper as he is making a series of dizzying post moves en route to a lay-up past a befuddled defender. But not even the Pointers had an idea what they were getting during the recruiting process.

Kalsow's college options following his senior year at Huntley (Ill.) High School were limited. UW-Green Bay asked Kalsow to walk on. Division II South Dakota State had interest. Kalsow even gave some thought to walking on at Northern Illinois.

His familiarity with the UWSP program came as a result of attending a Pointers basketball camp.

"When he came here I told him he reminded me of Larry Bird in his understanding and feel for the game. He was like `Really, because Larry Bird is my hero.' From the neck up, he's pretty darn good. As good as anybody," Bennett said.

"Is he a Division I (caliber) player now? Yes. I watch a lot of college games and there are a number of teams that can use the ton of things he brings to the table."

And Kalsow never needed a coach to tell him what areas of the game he needs to work on. He focused on his ball-handling in high school to the point where he became adept at bringing the ball up court.

Once he arrived on the UWSP campus it became obvious he had to bulk up and increase his strength in order to endure the bumping and banging that goes on in the paint in the WIAC. He even improved the range on his jumper.

"There are not too many people who want to battle with

DOUG WOJCIK

TOM CHAARLESWORTH

Above Left: Jason Kalsow is UWSP's all-time leader in scoring and rebounding.

Above Right: Head Coach Jack Bennett states, "Jason Kalsow is the most complete basketball player in the country at the Division III level."

Jason down low. He's extended his 3-point range and now it's like nobody knows how to guard him," UWSP's senior point guard Tamaris Relerford said. "He played point guard in high school, so that takes a lot of pressure off me. If teams press us full court, I can throw the ball back to him and not worry about it."

Teams may not have known much about Kalsow when he got to UWSP, but it didn't take long for him to make an impression. He started all 27 games as a freshman. By the time he was a sophomore, Kalsow was earning first-team All-WIAC accolades, a feat he repeated as a junior. This year, he is a Division III National Player of the Year candidate. So much for playing in anonymity.

"This was the place that fit me best. Joe Zuiker was graduating and that was the position I played," Kalsow said. "My biggest goal when I came here was just to play. College is a lot more about the mental game. I've learned when to post up or cut to the basket."

But Kalsow hasn't just made himself better during his time as a Pointer. Nick Bennett can vouch for the impact Kalsow has made on him and the rest of the Pointers.

The son of the Pointers coach has made a living on the perimeter throughout his career and ranks in the top 15 on the career scoring list. Without Kalsow around to attract double and triple teams in the post, Bennett's game would have been limited.

"When teams decide to play Kalsow one-on-one in the post he'll kill you. If they want to pack it in he's so unselfish he'll kick it out and find us," said Nick Bennett. "He's always been a really, really complete player."

Kalsow leads the Pointers in scoring, rebounds(6.9 a game), assists (41), steals (15) and blocked shots (16). As he has shown his versatility, Kalsow has also shown the ability to deliver in the clutch. Of the more than 1,400 points he has scored up to this stage in his college career one basket in particular will be forever etched in his memory.

Kalsow showed his mettle in pressure situations last spring in the national championship game. With the score tied and the Pointers in search of a hero, Kalsow stepped out of the phone booth. He drained a fade-away jumper as time expired to give the Pointers a thrilling 84-82 win over Williams (Mass.) College and their first Division III title in men's basketball.

"That'll be the shot I'll always remember. I can replay that shot over and over again," Kalsow said. "But we don't even get to that point if (Eric) Maus doesn't hit his shot against Lawrence or Nick doesn't hit some big 3-pointers."

That is a place Kalsow would like to visit again. He'd surely exchange all the school records and individual honors for another national title. Maybe then he can turn his attention to see if he has a future in professional basketball.

"As long as the team does well, individual awards are going to happen," Kalsow said. "I would like to look into it (the pros). It's something I would like to try just for the experience, if nothing else."

WISCONSIN
INTERCOLLEGIATE ATHLETIC CONFERENCE

Kalsow sets scoring record in wins

By Scott Williams

Top: Nick Bennett looks to post up Rob Dixon of Whitewater.

Below: Jason Kalsow banks in a runner against the Warhawks.

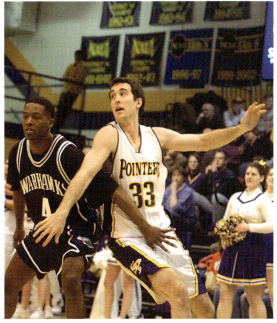

DOUG WOJCIK

DOUG WOJCIK

In a perfect world, the special night would have belonged entirely to Jason Kalsow.

Instead, Nick Bennett stole the show, and Kalsow and the rest of the University of Wisconsin-Stevens Point men's basketball team are happy he did.

Bennett scored 24 of his game-high 31 points in the second half as the second-ranked Pointers held off a charge by UW-Whitewater to secure a pivotal 75-64 victory at the Quandt Fieldhouse.

"Nick played a heck of a second half," Kalsow said. "They got us earlier in the year, so it was good to get them."

Kalsow did his part, finishing with 20 points to break the school's all-time career scoring record. He now has 1,661 points.

But it was Bennett who shot down the Warhawks' upset bid, and enabled the Pointers to maintain a share of the Wisconsin Intercollegiate Athletic Conference lead at 11-2. What made his performance even more impressive was the way Bennett rebounded after missing his first five shots.

"Nick had a monster second half with a capital 'M.' He absolutely carried us for long stretches of the half," UWSP coach Jack Bennett said. "He reminded me tonight of the roll he got on in the NCAA tournament last year."

Every time Whitewater (15-7, 7-7 WIAC) had the Pointers (19-2) on the ropes, Bennett knocked down a big basket. Despite a poor shooting night (37 percent), the Warhawks were able to gradually chip away at a 37-22 deficit early in the second half.

A better handle on the Pointers' troublesome 3-2 zone and some nearly flawless free throw shooting (24-for-28) allowed Whitewater to close the gap to 55-52 with 5:28 left.

"Their zone was very effective. We knew their length was going to be a problem. Our guards are quick but not that tall," Whitewater coach Pat Miller said. "Give Point credit. Every time we pushed them someone hit a big shot. We just got beat by a better team tonight."

The Warhawks have a history of staging big comebacks on the Quandt floor.

But Nick Bennett didn't leave anything to chance. Sure he drained his share of big 3-pointers - he was 5-for-7 from long range - during the crucial stages of the second half. Bennett was just as effective posting up Whitewater's smaller guards or cutting to the basket and converting old-fashioned three-point plays.

"I started off the game slow, but my coaches and teammates never got mad at me. I hit my final three shots of the first half and I guess that propelled me in the right direction," Nick Bennett said. "We have way too many good players on this team to rely on one person."

Good players who hit big shots at important times.

Take Brian Bauer for instance. The junior from Auburndale drilled his only basket - a 3-pointer - to close out the opening half and give the Pointers a 31-20 lead.

And don't forget Kyle Grusczynski, who buried a 3-pointer as the shot clock was winding down to make it 67-59 and all but seal the Warhawks' fate.

Then there is Kalsow who put an exclamation point of his special night with a thunderous dunk in the final minute.

"Everyone can and needs to step up when their number is called," coach Bennett said. "This was our biggest game up to this point in the season. We wanted this one so bad."

Left to Right:
- *Tamaris Relerford works against the Whitewater full-court pressure.*
- *All eyes are on the action as four starters-Jason Kalsow, Eric Maus, Nick Bennett and Tamaris Relerford--get a breather during the Whitewater game.*
- *The Kals-o Kounter.*
- *Coach Bennett congratulates senior Jason Kalsow on becoming the school's all-time leading scorer.*

POINTERS 75, WARHAWKS 64

UW-WHITEWATER (64) - Josh King 0-1 0-0 0, Angelo Griffin 4-5 6-9 14, Mike Toellner 3-5 3-3 10, Rob Dixon 3-7 6-6 14, Jeremy Manchester 1-7 7-8 9, Giovanni Riley 0-2 0-0 0, Craig Anderson 2-4 0-0 6, Jason Price 2-9 0-0 5, Melvin Williams 0-3 0-0 0, Rob Perry 2-3 2-2 6. Totals 17-46 24-28 64.

UW-STEVENS POINT (75) - Nick Bennett 10-17 6-7 31, Jason Kalsow 7-17 5-6 20, Eric Maus 1-3 2-2 4, Tamaris Relerford 0-3 2-3 2, Jon Krull 3-5 4-5 10, Steve Hicklin 0-1 0-0 0, Kyle Grusczynski 1-3 2-2 5, Brian Bauer 1-3 0-0 3, Gbenga Awe 0-1 0-0 0. Totals 23-53 21-25 75.

UW-Whitewater	20	44	- 64
UW-Stevens Point	31	44	- 75

3-point goals: Whitewater 6-20 (Toellner 1-1, Dixon 2-5, Manchester 0-1, Riley 0-2, Anderson 2-3, Price 1-7, Williams 0-1), Stevens Point 8-19 (Bennett 5-7, Kalsow 1-4, Relerford 0-2, Krull 0-1, Grusczynski 1-2, Bauer 1-3). Total fouls: Whitewater 21, Stevens Point 19. Fouled out: Manchester, Maus. Rebounds: Whitewater 33 (Griffin 7), Stevens Point 31 (Kalsow 10). Turnovers: Whitewater 16, Stevens Point 10. Att. - 2,519.

DOUG WOJCIK

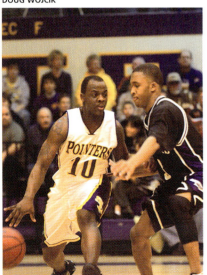

DOUG WOJCIK

DOUG WOJCIK

DOUG WOJCIK

FREE THROW
BRINGS END TO 18-YEAR-OLD RECORD

Below: Jason Kalsow shoots the free throw that will become his 1,650th point at UWSP—a new school record.

"He is absolutely the most complete player I've ever coached."

—*UWSP Head Coach Jack Bennett on Jason Kalsow*

By Scott Williams

DOUG WOJCIK

The names read like a who's who in the annals of University of Wisconsin-Stevens Point men's basketball.

Tim Naegeli, Terry Porter, Josh Iserloth and Tom Ritzenthaler just to name a few. All of them have to move over for Jason Kalsow.

With a free throw with 2:40 left in the first half Wednesday night, Kalsow became the Pointers all-time career scoring leader.

Kalsow finished with 20 points in the Pointers' 75-64 win over UW-Whitewater at the Quandt Fieldhouse to increase his total to 1,661. He surpassed Naegeli, who scored 1,649 points from 1983-87.

"It's a good feeling. It's a big achievement but I don't do it without my teammates, coaches and family," Kalsow said. "I wanted to get it out of the way, so I was a little anxious."

Kalsow got off to a quick start, scoring six of the first 12 points for UWSP. But the points became tougher to come by as the record grew nearer. Kalsow tied the record with a basket that gave the Pointers a 19-13 lead with 5:07 showing on the clock. The senior forward from Huntley (Ill.) then took an eraser to the record book when he sank the second of two free throws.

"I didn't know that was the free throw (to break the record)," Kalsow said. "The people of Stevens Point have been tremendous. To break it here makes it more special because I could share it with them."

Coincidentally, the recording-breaking night came against Whitewater, which just so happens to be the alma mater of his father Tom. His mother Donna was on hand to witness the accomplishment.

UWSP coach Jack Bennett has watched Kalsow throughout his four-year career and said nothing Kalsow accomplishes on the hardwood comes as a surprise.

"I think the record might have been weighing on him a little bit. It's such a significant record and I'm just so proud of him. He is absolutely the most complete player I've ever coached," Bennett said. "Now he can enjoy it."

In his typical humble manner, Kalsow was more concerned with picking up a victory than any record.

"It was real important we come out of here with a win. Seasons are too short to worry about records," Kalsow said. "I think more than the record, we'll be remembered as winners."

None of his predecessors scored two more important points than Kalsow, who drained the game-winning shot in the Division III national championship game.

Right now it's that title that Kalsow is more proud of than any record.

"Records are meant to be broken, but that national championship can't ever be taken away from us," Kalsow said.

WISCONSIN
INTERCOLLEGIATE ATHLETIC CONFERENCE

UWSP stays atop WIAC by beating Superior

Right: Steve Hicklin dives for a loose ball as Coach Bennett looks on.

DOUG WOJCIK

By Scott Williams

STEVENS POINT - The University of Wisconsin-Stevens Point men's basketball team wasn't in the mood for instant replay on Saturday night.

A year ago, UW-Superior cost the Pointers a share of the Wisconsin Intercollegiate Athletic Conference title by knocking them off in the final regular-season home game.

There would be no repeat this time around, as UWSP got on a roll in the second half and easily dispatched the Yellowjackets 83-58 at the Quandt Fieldhouse.

"Before the game we usually say something before the tip-off. Jason Kalsow said he didn't want to end our winning streak at home, and especially lose to Superior after last year," UWSP point guard Tamaris Relerford said.

With their 15th straight home victory, the second-ranked Pointers (20-2, 12-2 WIAC) placed themselves in prime position for a fifth WIAC title in six years.

Thanks to a helping hand from River Falls - which upended co-leader Platteville 60-59 - UWSP owns sole possession of first place in the conference standings with two games remaining.

The Pointers can clinch no worse than a share of the title with a win at home against River Falls on Wednesday.

"That is like Christmas and New Year's," said UWSP coach Jack Bennett after hearing the news Platteville got beat. "Now we need to take care of our end of the bargain. In a league as tough as this, a regular season title is something you always cherish."

With the pressure of breaking the school record behind him, Kalsow was unstoppable.

Kalsow scored a game-high 23 points on a nearly flawless 11-for-12 shooting from the field. He had plenty of help as Nick Bennett chipped in with 19 points and Tamaris Relerford had 13.

Relerford credited his productive night on the challenge of going up against Superior's Laron Reed, who he picked clean to spark a Pointer run in the first half.

"My defense is what gets my offense going. I knew I was against probably the quickest guard in the conference. Once I get a steal, I relax and play with more confidence," Relerford said.

Superior coach Jeff Kaminsky could only shake his head after taking a look at the rebounding statistics.

The numbers said it all: Stevens Point 37, Superior 22.

"Our problems to me were on the boards. That was the most disappointing element of the game for me. We played with zero toughness today," Kaminsky said. "We knew we were going to get out-skilled. So we had to out-tough them. We didn't win the physical battle."

Relerford hit a key 3-pointer in the closing seconds of the first half to put the Pointers on top 36-26.

The Yellowjackets (13-11, 4-11 WIAC) got off to a sluggish start after intermission, and UWSP took full advantage.

POINTERS 83, YELLOWJACKETS 58

UW-SUPERIOR (58) - Marc Rothschadl 5-9 0-1 11, Amin McDonald 2-4 1-2 5, Leonard Cobb 3-5 2-6 8, Laron Reed 5-11 3-5 16, Floyd Bayiha 1-2 4-6 7, Gus Couto 2-6 0-0 5, Courtney Collins 0-2 3-4 3, Arione Farrar 1-2 0-0 2, Kevin Turner 0-4 1-2 1. Totals 19-45 14-26 58.

UW-STEVENS POINT (83) - Nick Bennett 6-10 5-5 19, Jason Kalsow 11-12 0-0 23, Eric Maus 2-4 1-4 5, Tamaris Relerford 4-5 2-2 13, Jon Krull 3-6 0-0 6, Brett Hirsch 0-0 4-6 4, Brad Kalsow 1-2 4-4 6, Steve Hicklin 2-2 2-2 6, Kyle Grusczynski 0-3 0-0 0, Cory Krautkramer 0-2 0-2 0, Matt Bouche 0-1 1-2 1, Brian Bauer 0-0 0-1 0, Mike Prey 0-1 0-0 0, Gbenga Awe 0-2 0-0 0, Tyler Doyle 0-0 0-2 0. Totals 29-50 19-30 83.

UW-Superior	26	32	- 58
UW-Stevens Point	36	47	- 83

3-point goals: Superior 6-16 (Rothschadl 1-4, Reed 3-7, Bayiha 1-2, Couto 1-2, Turner 0-1), Stevens Point 6-15 (Bennett 2-6, J. Kalsow 1-1, Relerford 3-4, B. Kalsow 0-1, Grusczynski 0-3). Total fouls: Superior 25, Stevens Point 18. Fouled out: None. Rebounds: Superior 22 (Cobb 7), Stevens Point 37 (J. Kalsow 8). Turnovers: Superior 13, Stevens Point 8. Att. - 1,237.

WISCONSIN
INTERCOLLEGIATE ATHLETIC CONFERENCE

POINTERS PULVERIZE RIVER FALLS FOR TITLE
UWSP nails share of fifth crown in six years

By Scott Williams

Left: Jason Kalsow drains a three-pointer. Kalsow finished with a game-high 27 points.

DOUG WOJCIK

POINTERS 94, FALCONS 66

UW-RIVER FALLS (66) - Jeff Holt 2-7 4-4 8, Scott Kelly 2-4 1-2 7, Ryan Zylstra 4-4 0-0 8, Eric Kossoris 3-5 0-0 8, Hans Hoeg 3-7 4-4 12, Tyler Haag 0-0 1-2 1, Ryan Thompson 1-5 2-2 4, Nick Hall 1-1 1-2 4, Dan Torrez 2-5 0-0 6, Tim Pearson 0-3 0-0 0, Muris Lucarevic 4-8 0-0 8, Mitch Coffman 0-1 0-0 0, Cory Rondeau 0-1 0-0 0. Totals 22-51 13-16 66.

UW-STEVENS POINT (94) - Nick Bennett 5-12 0-0 13, Jason Kalsow 11-14 0-2 27, Eric Maus 5-5 3-3 13, Tamaris Relerford 5-6 1-2 16, Jon Krull 4-9 4-4 12, Brett Hirsch 2-2 0-0 4, Kyle Grusczynski 1-3 0-0 2, Mike Prey 1-2 0-0 2, Gbenga Awe 0-1 0-0 0, John Gleich 2-2 1-1 5. Totals 36-57 9-12 94.

UW-River Falls	37	29	- 66
UW-Stevens Point	42	52	- 94

3-point goals: River Falls 9-24 (Holt 0-4, Kelly 2-4, Kossoris 2-4, Hoeg 2-3, Thompson 0-3, Hall 1-1, Torrez 2-4, Tim Pearson 0-1), Stevens Point 13-24 (Bennett 3-8, J. Kalsow 5-6, Relerford 5-6, Krull 0-2, Grusczynski 0-2). Total fouls: River Falls 14, Stevens Point 14. Fouled out: none. Technical fouls: N. Bennett, J. Kalsow. Rebounds: River Falls 23 (Kossoris 5), Stevens Point 31 (J. Kalsow, Krull 7). Turnovers: River Falls 14, Stevens Point 8. Att. - 1,766.

The University of Wisconsin-River Falls men's basketball team had something UW-Stevens Point wanted - real bad.

It's called the Wisconsin Intercollegiate Athletic Conference regular-season crown.

After letting River Falls borrow it for a year, the Pointers went out Wednesday night and reclaimed what they feel is their rightful place on the throne.

UWSP secured at least a share of the WIAC title for the fifth time in the last six years with a devastating 94-66 victory on Senior Night at the Quandt Fieldhouse.

The Pointers can clinch the outright title with a win at Oshkosh on Saturday or a Platteville (12-3 WIAC) loss at Stout that night.

"When we set our goals before the season the first goal was to win the conference championship," said Eric Maus, one of six seniors on the roster. "This is the first step, and there is more to come."

Players always talk about being in a zone. Well, the entire Pointer team played like it was in the proverbial "zone" in the second half.

Three-point shots were raining down from all over the floor. Pinpoint passes led to easy baskets off sharp cuts. The culmination of the second-half fireworks were back-to-back explosive dunks by Jason Kalsow.

The Falcons (8-15, 4-11 WIAC) never knew what hit them.

"That was Pointer basketball at its best. We're a dangerous team when we're hitting on all cylinders," said Tamaris Relerford, another senior who tied a career high with 16 points on 5-for-5 shooting from behind the arc.

In a blink of an eye, what was a precarious 42-37 lead for UWSP at halftime turned into a full-fledged blowout. River Falls was helpless as the Pointers (21-2, 13-2 WIAC) put together a 28-7 blitz to take a commanding 70-44 advantage and the outcome was never in doubt again.

UWSP coach Jack Bennett called his team's performance after intermission "a clinic." He pointed to a smothering

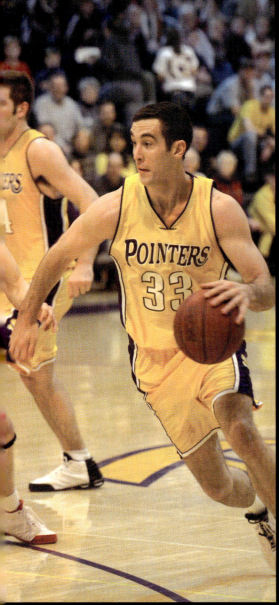

DOUG WOJCIK

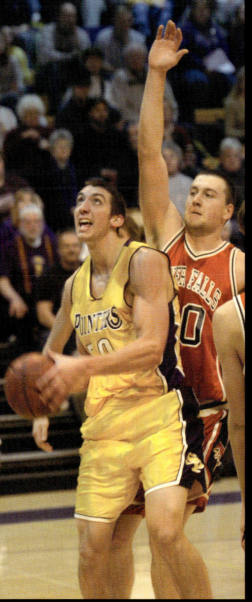

DOUG WOJCIK

Above Left: Nick Bennett dribbles past the River Falls defense.

Above Center: Eric Maus prepares to go up strong with an offensive rebound.

Right: A River Falls defender attempts to block a Nick Bennett three-pointer.

in-your-shorts defense as the catalyst.

"At halftime, I was not pleased with our defensive intensity. I challenged the guys and they came out with fire in their bellies," coach Bennett said. "We played the last 20 minutes like it was a national championship game. That was about as a good an offense as you'll see at this level."

All five starters finished in double figures for the Pointers, led by Kalsow with 27 points. Nick Bennett and Maus each chipped in with 13 points, while Jon Krull added 12.

UWSP's stretch of six-year dominance follows UW-Platteville's run of five straight championships from 1995-99. The Pointers won six consecutive titles from 1982-87.

"This senior class has been able to come out with some sort of championship every year. The WIAC championship eluded us last year, but we got the national championship," Relerford said.

An appreciative crowd said goodbye to Nick Bennett, Kalsow, Relerford, Kyle Grusczynski, Maus and John Gleich - all of whom found the scoring column.

"You dream about a night like this. We win a conference championship on Senior Night," coach Bennett said.

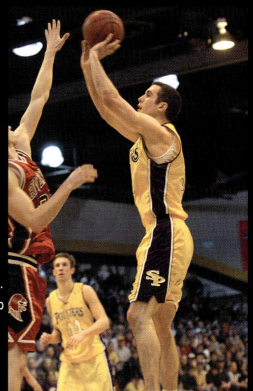

DOUG WOJCIK

POINTERS
MEET YOUNGER FANS

By Jill Steinke

DOUG WOJCIK

Above: Ashley Nickle dribbles in a game of PIG she and Hannah Jansch, left, were chosen to play in against Nick Bennett and Jason Kalsow, right, during a visit by the two with the fourth-and fifth graders at St. Stephen School.

"It was really cool because he is my favorite Pointer. I go to a lot of his games."

—10-year-old Caleb Finn on challenging Pointer All-American Nick Bennett to a dribbling match.

After winning a national championship, Pointer basketball stars Nick Bennett and Jason Kalsow are used to being questioned about their skills and their games in interviews or by their fans, but on Thursday they were asked some very different questions.

"What's your favorite pizza?" "Have you ever stuffed someone?" "Do you travel on the bus with reclining seats and a DVD player?" "Have you ever been to Florida?"

Fourth- and fifth-graders at St. Stephen's Elementary School got to ask the basketball players all sorts of questions when Bennett and Kalsow visited the school. Some of the students also got to compete against the University of Wisconsin-Stevens Point players in a round of PIG and ball handling.

Caleb Finn, 10, took on Bennett in a dribbling match, which was like a dream come true. "It was really cool because he is my favorite Pointer," Finn said with a huge grin. "I go to a lot of his games."

Fans like Finn in the community are what make playing in Stevens Point exciting. Bennett and Kalsow are using their school visits to repay their loyal fans. "It's important to do stuff for the community," Bennett said. "It's fun to see the kids. They come to our games and cheer."

The students were cheering loudly on Thursday on the small elementary school basketball court as Bennett and Kalsow demonstrated some of their abilities, including Kalsow's slam dunk and Bennett's perfect jump shot.

It was pretty cool to see their moves, 11-year-old Alexa Marsicek said. A basketball player herself, she watched their moves closely to find things she might try and listened intently to their advice to aspiring athletes.

"They gave good advice to practice hard," she said.

The Pointers advised the students that if they worked hard at whatever they want to do, they will achieve it. Bringing that message to area students is Kalsow's way of thanking his supporters.

"It's the least we could do for them," he said.

WISCONSIN
INTERCOLLEGIATE ATHLETIC CONFERENCE

Oshkosh upsets Pointer men

By Larry Graham

Right: Kyle Grusczynski drives past UW-Oshkosh guard Andy Jahnke.

PHOTOS COURTESY OF UW-OSHKOSH SPORTS INFORMATION OFFICE

OSHKOSH - The University of Wisconsin-Oshkosh men's basketball team's scoring tendencies have been somewhat erratic lately. That's not a good sign going into a matchup against one of the top teams in the country.

"We knew we had to shoot the ball well. That's how everybody's pulling upsets at this time of year," Titans basketball coach Ted Van Dellen said.

The Titans drained 10 3-pointers in a 74-59 upset win over Stevens Point on Saturday at Kolf Sports Center.

The loss denied the Pointers, ranked No. 1 in NCAA Division III according to D3hoops.com, the outright title in the Wisconsin Intercollegiate Athletic Conference.

"It shows the character of the team. We were playing for our 18th win and we talked about climbing up the ladder and keeping the tradition," Van Dellen said. "They really played a whale of a ballgame."

An avalanche of 3-point plays led to the Titans' lead. UWO earned its first lead of the game on a 3-point play by Kerry Gibson when he was fouled on a field goal and made the free throw.

Stevens Point retaliated with a three-pointer by Brian Bauer, before consecutive three-pointers by Jim Capelle, Andy Jahnke and Kyle Johnson.

"That was definitely key because you can't let them back in a ball game," Van Dellen said.

UWO led the entire second half. An 8-0 run early resulted in a 51-35 Titans' advantage.

"As the time winds down and you're down double digits, boy that's a bear," Van Dellen said. "It puts a little pressure on you and even a good team like them had a hard time handling the pressure of being down double digits."

Jahnke led all scorers with 24 points with Gibson scoring 17 and senior Andy Fernholz adding 15. Jason Kalsow paced the Pointers with 23 points.

The win avenges a 69-44 loss to the Pointers earlier in the season.

"Anytime you beat a team like Stevens Point, it's a heck of a feather in your hat," Van Dellen said. "Now, it's a new season and it's going to be very interesting."

POINTERS 59, TITANS 74

UW-STEVENS POINT (21-3, 13-3) - Jon Krull 0 2-2 2, Jason Kalsow 7 7-7 23, Eric Maus 3 0-0 6, Tamaris Relerford 1 0-0 2, Nick Bennett 4 3-3 12, Kyle Grusczynski 2 2-2 8, Brian Bauer 1 0-0 3, Gbenga Awe 0 3-4 3 Totals 18 17-18.

UW-OSHKOSH (18-7, 11-5) - Jim Cappelle 1 0-1 3, Kerry Gibson 6 5-5 17, Andy Fernholz 4 5-6 15, Chad Doedens 1 0-0 2, Andy Jahnke 6 8-8 24, Kyle Johnson 3 0-0 9, Nathan Wesener 1 0-0 2, Pete Warning 0 2-2 2, Totals 22 20-22, 74.

UW-Stevens Point	32	27	- 56
UW-Oshkosh	43	31	- 74

3-point goals - UWO 10 (Capelle, Fernholz 2, Jahnke 4, K. Johnson 3), UWSP 6 (Kalsow 2, Bennett 1, Grusczynski 2). Fouled out - Kalsow. Total fouls - UWO 17, UWSP 20. Rebounds - UWO 36 (Gibson 9), UWSP 25 (Kalsow 6). Assists - UWO 14 (Fernholz 6), UWSP 7 (Bennett 4).

WIAC TOURNAMENT

POINTERS SPREAD IT AROUND IN WIN
Kalsow breaks rebound record

By Scott Williams

Left: Nick Bennett and Eric Maus pressure Superior's Amin McDonald.

DOUG WOJCIK

POINTERS 88, YELLOWJACKETS 68

UW-SUPERIOR (68) - Kevin Turner 0-5 0-0 0, Leonard Cobb 7-11 5-6 19, Laron Reed 6-17 4-5 21, Floyd Nyemeck Bayiha 6-11 3-3 16, Marc Rothschadl 3-9 0-0 8, Gus Couto 0-1 0-0 0, Courtney Collins 0-1 0-0 0, Amin McDonald 1-5 0-0 2, Arione Farrar 1-2 0-0 2. Totals 24-62 12-14 68.

UW-STEVENS POINT (88) - Jon Krull 6-8 8-8 20, Jason Kalsow 5-8 0-0 11, Eric Maus 5-7 4-4 14, Tamaris Relerford 2-2 1-2 5, Nick Bennett 8-14 4-4 22, Brett Hirsch 1-1 0-0 2, Brad Kalsow 0-0 1-2 1, Steve Hicklin 2-3 0-0 4, Kyle Grusczynski 2-5 0-1 4, Cory Krautkramer 0-1 0-0 0, Brian Bauer 1-1 0-0 2, Gbenga Awe 1-1 1-2 3. Totals 33-51 19-23 88.

UW-Superior	23	45	- 68
UW-Stevens Point	39	49	- 88

3-point goals: Superior 8-22 (Reed 5-10, Bayiha 1-3, Rothschadl 2-8, Couto 0-1), Stevens Point 3-10 (J. Kalsow 1-1, Bennett 2-6, Hicklin 0-1, Grusczynski 0-2). Total fouls: Superior 19, Stevens Point 14. Fouled out: none. Technical foul: Superior coach Kaminsky. Rebounds: Superior 30 (Redd, McDonald 7), Stevens Point 30 (J. Kalsow 7). Turnovers: Superior 16, Stevens Point 15. Att. - 1,237.

Jon Krull and Eric Maus might want to get the "Thank You" notes in the mail after their Wisconsin Intercollegiate Athletic Conference quarterfinal men's basketball game Tuesday night.

Thanks to a highlight reel on the fine art of the extra pass produced by the University of Wisconsin-Stevens Point men's basketball team, the so-called "role players" busted out.

Maus and Krull were on the receiving end of many of those passes, and the Pointers went on to rout UW-Superior 88-68 at Quandt Fieldhouse.

Krull and Maus finished with season-highs of 20 and 14 points, respectively, as third-ranked UWSP earned a semifinal home date with Oshkosh on Thursday.

"When we start passing the ball like that the other teams don't know who is going to score for us, and that makes it difficult to guard us," Krull said.

The Pointers (22-3) were closing in on breaking the all-time WIAC tournament record for assists by a team until garbage time set in. At one point in the second half UWSP had assists on 22 of the team's first 25 field goals. Ultimately, the team finished with 24 assists, tying Oshkosh (2003) for second most. La Crosse had 26 assists in a game with Whitewater in 2000.

It's that better-to-give-than-to-receive philosophy that helped carry the Pointers to the Division III national title a year ago. And was missing in a loss at Oshkosh last Saturday.

"Against Oshkosh we didn't make the extra pass. Everyone on this team is capable of scoring, so somebody is usually open," said Jason Kalsow, who handed out a team-high seven assists to go with 11 points and seven rebounds.

As a result of the unselfish attitude, the Pointers finished the night shooting 65 percent (33 for 51) from the field. Of course, those types of shooting percentages would be inevitable when Superior (14-12) treats defense like an afterthought. The Yellowjackets employed on the ball pressure, but displayed a matador defense

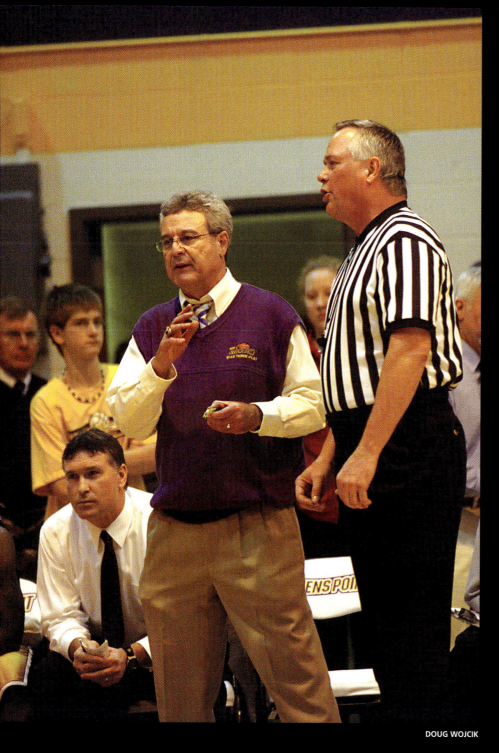
Above: Coach Bennett discusses the physical play with official Bob Zahradka.

around the basket for most of the night.

"This was not a fun time. I thought our defense let us down a lot," Superior coach Jeff Kaminsky said. "The game is not that complicated. They broke us down too much. Ultimately, our defense on the help side didn't do a very good job."

The night was also a historic one for the Pointers. Kalsow ripped up his second page of the UWSP record book this season when he grabbed a rebound with 4:30 left in regulation. He now has 823 for his career, surpassing the 46-year old record of 821 held by La Vern Luebstorf. Earlier in the season, Kalsow broke the school's all-time career scoring record.

"That is a real special record because it stood longer than the other one. And it's a great feeling to come out and know I just didn't do one thing on the court," Kalsow said.

Nick Bennett, who finished with a game-high 22 points, erased another page in the record book when he nailed a 3-pointer at 10:52 of the opening half. That was the 205th of his career, breaking the mark of 204 set by Andy Boario.

The shot gave the Pointers a commanding 23-7 lead. The Yellowjackets would get no closer than 10 points the rest of the game.

"Superior creates the most turnovers in the league, so you have to take care of the ball and pass well," UWSP coach Jack Bennett said. "I hope people appreciate when we pass the ball well. We chopped apart their defense for lay-up after lay-up."

There came a point in the second half when the outcome took a back seat to making sure the players came out of the game healthy. Since nothing else was working, Superior decided to test the manhood of the Pointers, who refused to back down. A good sign according to their coach.

"That was good for us. That kind of physical play will prepare us for later in the tournament," coach Bennett said.

Top: Senior Nick Bennett looks to catch-and-shoot versus UW-Oshkosh in WIAC tournament action.

Below: Jon Krull puts his patented spin move on UW-Oshkosh's Andy Jahnke.

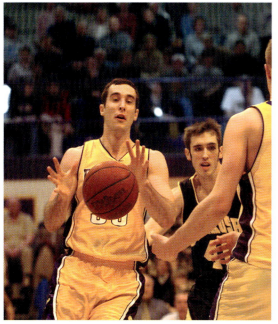

DOUG WOJCIK

DOUG WOJCIK

WIAC TOURNAMENT

NO PLACE LIKE HOME
Pointers defeat Oshkosh, will host WIAC title game Saturday

By Nathan Vine

When an opposing men's basketball team takes on the University of Wisconsin-Stevens Point, according to UW-Oshkosh coach Ted Van Dellen, the majority of your worries come down to two players.

"Don't get me wrong, they have a great supporting group of players, but it all comes down to Jason Kalsow and Nick Bennett," Van Dellen said. "Those are two fabulous players, and you win games at this time of the year with guys like that."

Van Dellen's fears came true Thursday night as the senior duo each came up big in the second half to lead the No. 2-seeded Pointers to a 65-59 victory over the No. 3-seed Titans in the semifinals of the WIAC Tournament at Quandt Fieldhouse.

The victory, only five days removed from a 74-59 loss to the Titans in Oshkosh, came with a dose of added excitement. UWSP will now host Saturday's conference title game against UW-Whitewater, who knocked off top-seeded UW-Platteville 89-76 Thursday.

"This felt a lot like last year when we thought we beat Oshkosh here in the semis, and I was getting our team ready to go to River Falls and we ended up here against Platteville," UWSP coach Jack Bennett said. "I give Oshkosh a lot of credit, because they played a heck of a ball game. This was a Final Four-quality contest."

Bennett and Kalsow remained calm under pressure and came up with the biggest plays for the Pointers (23-3). Bennett, who needed just 12 points to pass Brant Bailey for seventh place on the school's all-time scoring list, scored 16 of his game-high 28 points in the second half. The senior connected on all four of his free throw attempts in the final 2 minutes, 56 seconds of the game to help break a 55-55 deadlock.

"The WIAC is as tough as it comes," coach Bennett said. "Oshkosh didn't lose this game tonight, we just happened to make a couple of more shots than they did. It reminded me a lot of the national championship game last year."

Meanwhile Kalsow, who scored nine of his 12 points in the second half, hit on two free throws of his own and set up the winning field goal when, after drawing two Oshkosh defenders off the dribble, he found Eric Maus open under the basket for a layup that pushed the Pointers' lead to 63-59.

Prior to that, the Titans (19-8) seemed to have an

answer for every one of the Pointers' shots. After shooting just 29 percent (8 of 27) in the first half, including a combined 1 for 13 shooting performance by leading scorers Jim Capelle and Andy Jahnke, UW-Oshkosh connected on seven 3-pointers in the second half and took the lead on four different occasions.

"It was a heck of a ball game," UW-Oshkosh senior guard Andy Fernholz said. "Both teams were up and down in the second half, and they (UWSP) made some big plays at the end."

Asked whether the Pointers had solidified themselves a position in the NCAA Division III National Tournament regardless of Saturday's contest, Coach Bennett answered almost immediately.

"Yes I do," he said. "I thought tonight was the big game for us, and based on what we have done all year long in games like this we should be in. We'd like to go in through the front door, but Whitewater is going to come in here very loose, and it's going to be a tough game between two good teams."

Left to Right:
- Long time Pointer supporter Jack Porter (left) and former Stevens Point Journal sports editor Don Friday enjoy the action from the front row.
- Eric Maus plays tough defense against talented Oshkosh big man Kerry Gibson.
- Head Coach Jack Bennett takes a moment to relax on the bench.

POINTERS 65, TITANS 59

UW-OSHKOSH (59) - Jim Capelle 4-14 2-2 13, Andy Jahnke 6-15 0-0 15, Kerry Gibson 5-10 3-5 13, Andy Fernholz 2-7 0-0 6, Chad Doedens 3-5 0-0 6, Nathan Wesener 1-1 0-0 2, Pete Warning 1-2 2-2 4. Totals 22-54 7-9 59.

UW-STEVENS POINT (65) - Jon Krull 2-3 1-2 5, Jason Kalsow 4-10 4-5 12, Eric Maus 3-6 4-4 10, Tamaris Relerford 2-3 0-0 5, Nick Bennett 8-14 8-8 28, Kyle Grusczynski 0-5 2-2 2, Brian Bauer 1-1 1-1 3. Totals 20-42 20-22 65.

UW-Oshkosh	18	41	- 59
UW-Stevens Point	23	42	- 65

3-point goals: Oshkosh 8-21 (Capelle 3-9, Jahnke 3-8, Gibson 0-1, Fernholz 2-3), Stevens Point 5-14 (Kalsow 0-2, Relerford 1-2, Bennett 4-7, Grusczynski 0-3). Total fouls: Oshkosh 14, Stevens Point 13. Fouled out: none. Rebounds: Oshkosh 27 (Fernholz 7), Stevens Point 26 (Kalsow, Maus 7). Turnovers: Oshkosh 8, Stevens Point 8. Att. - 1,953.

DOUG WOJCIK

DOUG WOJCIK

DOUG WOJCIK

WIAC TOURNAMENT

Pointers win WIAC Crown
UWSP locks up automatic bid in NCAA tournament

By Scott Williams

Left: Nick Bennett drives baseline for two of his 16 points.

DOUG WOJCIK

STEVENS POINT - The University of Wisconsin-Stevens Point men's basketball team can forget about finding the back door or a side door to the NCAA Tournament. Instead, the Pointers barreled through the front door with a battering ram - a.k.a. Jason Kalsow.

Kalsow powered his way to a game-high 28 points to lead four players in double digits and UWSP claimed its second straight WIAC Tournament title with an 87-77 win over UW-Whitewater on Saturday before an overflow crowd of 2,550 at Quandt Fieldhouse.

UWSP - now 24-3 and the defending NCAA Division III national champions - will learn who their first opponent will be tonight when the brackets are announced. The opening round of the tournament is Thursday.

As far as Kalsow was concerned, there was never a thought of leaving their season in the hands of the Division III selection committee.

"Personally, I did think that way, and there was no talk about that in the locker room," he said. "We didn't want another WIAC team in and possibly have to deal with them again."

Every possible entry into the NCAA Tournament was boarded up for the Warhawks, who finished 19-9.

Whitewater may have felt there was a crack in the front door after Mike Toellner slammed down a basket off transition with 14:11 left in the second half to put it on top 56-54.

But that door slammed shut as the Pointers immediately went on a decisive 17-5 run over the next 4:53 to grab a 71-61 lead.

"This was the type of score we wanted. We felt if it was close at the 10-minute mark we would be in a good position to take the game over," said Whitewater coach Pat Miller, whose team was denied a 13th trip to the national tournament and first since 1997. "They responded like the defending national champions, basically."

The up-tempo nature of the game played right into the hands of the Warhawks.

With nine players seeing at least 10 minutes of action, the plan was to try to wear down a Pointer team lacking that sort of depth.

There would be no indication of a fade by UWSP, however. In fact, just the opposite was true as the regular season co-champions turned up the

POINTERS 87, WARHAWKS 77

UW-WHITEWATER (77) - Angelo Griffin 3-9 2-2 8, Mike Toellner 3-5 0-0 6, Craig Anderson 6-13 10-16 25, Jeremy Manchester 1-6 0-0 2, Melvin Williams 7-13 2-3 18, Giovanni Riley 1-3 1-2 3, Rob Dixon 0-3 0-0 0, Jason Price 2-6 0-0 5, Josh King 1-1 2-2 4, Rob Perry 2-4 2-3 6. Totals 26-63 19-28 77.

UW-STEVENS POINT (87) - Jon Krull 3-8 5-5 11, Jason Kalsow 11-15 4-9 28, Eric Maus 3-5 2-2 8, Tamaris Relerford 2-5 6-9 12, Nick Bennett 4-10 6-8 16, Steve Hicklin 1-1 0-0 2, Kyle Grusczynski 4-6 0-1 9, Brian Bauer 0-2 0-0 0, Gbenga Awe 0-0 1-2 1. Totals 28-52 24-36 87.

UW-Whitewater	43	34 -	77
UW-Stevens Point	47	40 -	87

3-point goals: Whitewater 6-22 (Toellner 0-1, Anderson 3-8, Manchester 0-1, Williams 2-7, Dixon 0-2, Price 1-3), Stevens Point 7-17 (Krull 0-2, Kalsow 2-4, Relerford 2-3, Bennett 2-5, Grusczynski 1-2, Bauer 0-1). **Total fouls:** Whitewater 25, Stevens Point 16. **Fouled out:** Manchester. **Technical foul:** Whitewater bench. **Rebounds:** Whitewater 34 (Toellner 7), Stevens Point 33 (Kalsow 10). **Turnovers:** Whitewater 11, Stevens Point 13. **Att.** - 2,550.

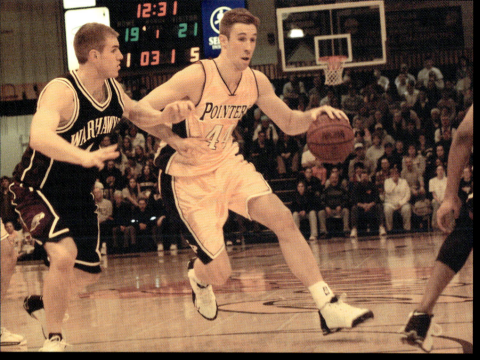

DOUG WOJCIK

Whitewater's inside-outside duo of senior Angelo Griffin and Jeremy Manchester were held to eight and two points, respectively. "The watershed moment of the game was when they went up by two (56-54). I called a time-out and challenged our guys to suck it up," Pointer coach Jack Bennett said. "We had to draw a line in the sand and get the game back to our tempo."

Senior Tamaris Relerford and Kyle Grusczynski showed off their artistic nature in the form of crucial 3-point baskets during the run.

Relerford hit a pair of long-range bombs and Grusczynski added another during the decisive second-half charge.

"I think you run a big risk when you concentrate on shutting down (Nick) Bennett and Kalsow. Their supporting players are very good," Miller said. "It comes down to what poison do you want?"

Neither team enjoyed more than a seven-point advantage at any point over the first 34 minutes.

With Griffin and Manchester held in check, the Warhawks turned to Craig Anderson and Melvin Williams to keep them within striking distance. Anderson finished with 25 points and Williams added 18.

"I thought we got swept up in the Whitewater speed game," coach Bennett said.

That is until Relerford and Grusczynski started firing away from the perimeter.

Forced to get out on the shooters, Whitewater left the lane open for business for Kalsow, who went to work in the post-up. He scored 10 of his points during a 7-minute span in the second half with the game still in doubt.

"Once 'T' (Relerford), Kyle and Nick start hitting threes that opens the middle for me," Kalsow said.

Top Left: Jason Kalsow led all scorers with 28 points.

Left: Tamaris Relerford sneaks into the lane for two against Whitewater.

DOUG WOJCIK

NCAA DIVISION III
BASKETBALL TOURNAMENT

THE OPENING TIP-OFF
UWSP's defense of national title begins against Lawrence

By Scott Williams

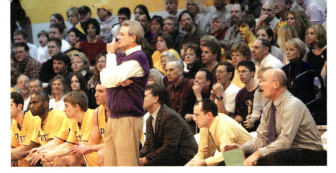

DOUG WOJCIK

Above: Head Coach Jack Bennett leads his squad into the NCAA tournament. The Pointers play a Lawrence team they beat in last year's tourney 82-81 in overtime.

All of the waiting and uncertainty is over.

The defending NCAA Division III national champion University of Wisconsin-Stevens Point men's basketball team will open defense of its title against Lawrence University.

Lawrence (20-5) earned a date with the top-ranked Pointers (24-3) after knocking off Gustavus Adolphus 70-56 in an opening-round showdown Thursday in St. Peter, Minn.

"It'll be a battle," UWSP coach Jack Bennett said. "They certainly outplayed Gustavus Adolphus. They were very impressive in that win."

The teams are hardly strangers to one another. All the Pointers and Lawrence have to do is look back to the Elite Eight last year when the teams played one of the classic games in the NCAA tournament.

Nick Bennett hit a 3-pointer with 10 seconds left to force overtime, and Eric Maus supplied the nail in the Vikings coffin with a late jumper in an 82-81 Pointer win in Tacoma, Wash.

UWSP leads the all-time series 23-11 in the oldest rivalry in school history. The Pointers played Lawrence in their first two games as a varsity program in 1897.

"They were one point away from the Final Four last season," Pointer senior forward Jason Kalsow said. "I think a lot of teams take them for granted. People look at the Midwest Conference and don't think it's a powerhouse.

"This is going to be a typical NCAA back-and-forth game. It's going to come down to who toughs it out."

Any thoughts of overlooking the Vikings may be catastrophic. Lawrence won the regular season championship in the Midwest Conference and knocked off Ripon 82-77 in overtime for the tournament title.

Need more proof of just how formidable the Vikings are? Just ask UW-Oshkosh and Wisconsin Intercollegiate Athletic Conference co-champion UW-Platteville - both of whom lost to the Vikings on their home courts this season.

"At this stage there are no favorites and no upsets," Bennett said. "These are 32 of the best teams out of a pool of something like 400 in Division III. It's a bunch of great teams battling it out to see who advances."

In certain respects, the Pointers and the Vikings mirror each another. Each team boasts tremendous balance inside and out. Chris Braier, a 6-foot-4 workhorse of a power forward, supplies the bulk - literally and figuratively - on the inside. He averages 15.4 points and 11.6 rebounds, the latter ranking 12th nationally.

"He really complements their guards. We can't let him kill us on the offensive glass. He has a sense of where shots are going," said Kalsow, who will likely be matched up with Braier for much of tonight's game.

"He's the real deal."

Should the Pointers pay too much attention to Braier, there are a number of perimeter players who can do some serious damage. Jason Hollinbeck, Dan Evans and Kyle MacGillis all average in double figures.

Lawrence showed just how dangerous it can be from 3-point range in last year's game with Pointers, draining 15 shots from behind the arc. UWSP would like to make things a little tougher on the Vikings' outside shooters this time around, according to Bennett.

"I'm hoping our defense is better. I would like for us to make it a little tougher on them to score. They pass the ball extremely well," he said. "They're not a mirror image of us, but I think philosophically we're very similar."

The Pointers are hoping to avoid a similar outcome as the last time they received an opening-round bye. Gustavus Adolphus came to town for a second round game in 2002-03, and the Gusties ended the Pointers season 75-62 at Quandt.

In an effort to avoid a repeat performance, UWSP has gone very hard in practice in an effort to maintain the competitive edge it had coming out of winning the WIAC tournament.

"We've kept things real intense in practice so we keep that edge you should have going into the tournament," senior point guard Tamaris Relerford said. "We're familiar with being in the position of everyone gearing for us."

In a game where every little intangible might be multiplied by a 100, the Pointers feel fortunate to be playing the game at home.

UWSP owns a 15-0 record at Quandt this season. The game is a sell out. All 2,787 seats are taken, and approximately only 250 of those are reserved for Lawrence fans.

In the same respect, the Vikings are hardly intimidated on the road. They have gone into places like Platteville, Oshkosh and Gustavus Adolphus, and come home with wins.

"We fought for this all year. Hopefully, we can cash our chips in. This year in all my years here is the best we've been on our home court. I like our crowd," Bennett said.

"I really believe this is the premier game in the nation at this stage of the tournament."

NCAA DIVISION III BASKETBALL TOURNAMENT

POINTER MANIA
Parents put on plenty of miles

By Kelly McBride

TOM CHARLESWORTH

Above: Cindy Lee, mother of Pointer guard Shawn, lets everyone know how she feels about Pointer basketball.

It's 199 miles from the Kalsow home in Huntley, Ill., to the Quandt Fieldhouse on the University of Wisconsin-Stevens Point campus.

But for Tom and Donna Kalsow, parents of Pointer hoopsters Jason and Brad Kalsow, making the nearly 400-mile round-trip in a single evening and then getting up with the sun for work is more than worth it.

They're just two of myriad Pointer parents so dedicated to watching their sons take to the court they'll sacrifice vacation days, gallons of fuel and precious sleep to travel the state and beyond following their favorite team. As the Pointers suit up to face Lawrence University at 7 p.m. today, some of their most dedicated fans will once again be in the crowd as they work to defend their NCAA Division III national crown.

"We're so used to (the drive), it doesn't even bother us anymore," said Donna Kalsow. "Now it's just second nature. We wouldn't trade it for anything."

Playing games relatively closer to home so parents can attend regularly - though it still may be a bit of a drive - is one of the benefits of Division III basketball, said Pointer assistant coach Bob Semling.

"There's no question," he said. "It really is a huge lift for the guys to be able to play in front of their parents and to have them be part of their careers."

That's certainly the case for senior guard Tamaris Relerford, who said his parents always have been there to cheer him after wins and console him after losses. On the rare occasion they couldn't make a game, Relerford said they'd always follow up by phone.

Relerford's dad, Roy Bolton, never saw the support as anything but enjoyable. Like other Pointer parents, he's become accustomed to the two hour-plus drive from Beloit.

"It's really been a blessing," Bolton said. "It's a pleasurable ride from Beloit to Stevens Point. I really want to thank the people of Stevens Point for supporting our son."

For many Pointers and their parents, the game-day routine is much the same: Arrive just in time for tip-off, cheer like crazy for four quarters of basketball, take the hungry

> "We're so used to (the drive), it doesn't even bother us anymore. We wouldn't trade it for anything."
>
> —Donna Kalsow, mother of Brad and Jason Kalsow on traveling from Illinois to watch her sons play.

Above: Sue Bennett, wife of Jack and mother of Nick, is a fixture at every Pointer game.

TOM CHARLESWORTH

players for a post-game meal and hit the road. But for some parents, game-day superstitions have become part of the repertoire.

Following a loss to UW-Oshkosh during which she wore red and black, Kathy Grusczynski - mom of senior guard Kyle - has sworn off the colors and now sticks strictly to purple and gold for game day. She's attended games with the family of Kyle's girlfriend in which everyone dons purple boas and handmade Pointer bracelets. Tom Kalsow had a picture he used to rub for luck. After last year's NCAA tourney run, however, the picture wore out and he had to get a new one.

And the family support doesn't exist strictly within blood-related kin. All of the players and parents have bonded into a supportive community, said Barb Maus, mother of senior center Eric.

"To see the parents come up to Eric and for us to go up to the other guys, too, after the game - it's just become such a big family affair," she said.

Knowing their parents are watching is a plus for all the Pointers, Relerford said.

"It feels good," Relerford said. "You look in the stands, (and) you might see 1,000, 2,000 people. But you can always find your parents."

NCAA DIVISION III BASKETBALL TOURNAMENT

OFF AND RUNNING
Pointers start title defense with win

By Scott Williams

Top: The starting five prior to introductions.

Below: All eyes are on Jason Kalsow as he shoots a three-pointer.

TOM KUJAWSKI

STEVENS POINT - Lawrence University made a big mistake in its NCAA Division III men's basketball tournament second-round game Saturday night.

Actually, the problem happened nearly 365 days ago when the Vikings played the University of Wisconsin-Stevens Point in the Elite Eight.

That familiarity bred success for the top-ranked Pointers, who opened defense of their national championship with a 79-45 thrashing of Lawrence in front of a full house at the Quandt Fieldhouse.

UWSP (25-3) will play Puget Sound (Wash.) in sectional action next Friday at a site and time to be determined today. Puget Sound defeated Buena Vista (La.) 85-82 on Saturday night.

"I think our game with them last season got our attention," UWSP coach Jack Bennett said.

So did the 15 3-pointers the Vikings rained down on UWSP last season. So did the 40 points Lawrence put up in the first half a year ago. And the Pointers weren't too thrilled to see 81 on the Vikings side of the scoreboard at the end of last season's game.

Bennett had a little better defense from his team at the top of the wish list. How about a lot better defense?

"I would say our defense was 100 percent better this year," Bennett said. "We'll do whatever we have to do on defense to give us the best chance to win."

In the tournament opener, that meant an in-your-face mind-set in the man-to-man. Then the Pointers sprung their secret weapon - a 3-2 zone that has baffled teams all season.

You can add the Vikings to the list of discombobulated teams. They endured scoring droughts of 5:17 in the first half and nearly seven minutes in the second half.

Lawrence watched its number of 3-pointers cut from 15 to seven in a matter of a year, and managed only 38 field-goal attempts the entire game. You can even toss in a couple shot-clock violations for more proof of

TOM KUJAWSKI

Above: Sophomore guard Brett Hirsch drives baseline against the Lawrence defense.

TOM KUJAWSKI

how stingy the UWSP defense was on this night.

"When they were in the 3-2 zone, it looked like we hadn't worked on it in years," Lawrence coach John Tharp said. "We got handled in every single aspect of the game tonight. We happened to play a bad game against the best team in the country and it showed."

The Pointers probably considered themselves fortunate to hold a 36-26 lead at halftime with leading scorer Jason Kalsow held to three first-half points. He finished with 15.

Jon Krull also helped to pick up the slack with 13 points, and provided the Pointers with some added muscle in the paint to offset the slow start by Kalsow.

It doesn't hurt to have Nick Bennett in a zone. The senior guard came out on fire, connecting on 7 of 10 shots from the field.

Superstitious or not, Bennett's pre-game meditation routine worked wonders as he scored a game-high 23.

"That's my routine that I've done every game since my freshman season," said Bennett, who heads to the solitude of the UWSP bench during the final minutes of warm-ups to spend some alone time deep in thought. "A little relaxation before I go to battle."

The first half simply turned out to be the calm before the storm.

Once the Pointers shook off some of the competitive rust from a week layoff, the offensive execution caught up with the defense.

That meant only one thing for Lawrence - lights out.

UWSP opened the second half with a 23-5 run over the opening 7:25 to end any thoughts of a Vikings comeback, and turned the game into a laugher.

"In the second half we felt if we got them on their heels, we could wear them down," said Bennett, referring to a road-weary Vikings team that played a first-round game at Gustavus Adolphus on Thursday. "We had to deliver the first punch and see if their legs got weary."

Left to Right:
- *Nick Bennett hits another three-pointer.*
- *The Pointer defense held Lawrence to just 19 second-half points.*
- *Jason Kalsow looks to score against Chris Braier of Lawrence. Kalsow finished with 15 points.*
- *Steve Hicklin handles the Lawrence pressure. Hicklin was called to action after senior point guard Tamaris Relerford went down with an injury.*

POINTERS 79, VIKINGS 45

Lawrence (45): Brendan Falls 3-8 0-1 9, Chris Braier 3-8 1-4 7, Matt Osland 1-1 0-0 2, Jason Holinbeck 1-5 0-0 2, Dan Evans 3-6 1-2 10, Brett Sjoberg 0-2 0-1 0, Ben Rosenblatt 1-3 1-2 4, Kyle MacGillis 1-4 1-2 3, Keven Bradley 0-0 2-2 2, Nate Dineen 0-0 2-2 2, Tony Olson 1-1 0-0 2, Ryan Wendel 0-0 2-2 2. FG: 14-38. FT: 10-18.

UWSP (79): Jon Krull 4-5 4-4 13, Jason Kalsow 5-9 4-4 15, Eric Maus 3-8 2-2 8, Tamaris Relerford 0-3 2-2 2, Nick Bennett 9-13 1-1 23, Shawn Lee 1-1 2-2 5, Brett Hirsch 1-1 1-2 3, Brad Kalsow 0-1 0-0 0, Steve Hicklin 2-3 1-2 5, Kyle Grusczynski 0-1 3-4 3, Brian Bauer 1-1 0-0 2, Gbenga Awe 0-2 0-0 0. FG: 26-48. FT: 20-23.

Lawrence University 26 19 - 45
UW-Stevens Point   36 43 - 79

3-point goals: Lawrence 7-21 (Falls 3-6, Braier 0-1, Holinbeck 0-4, Evans 3-4, Sjoberg 0-2, Rosenblatt 1-2, MacGillis 0-2), Stevens Point 7-17 (Krull 1-1, J. Kalsow 1-2, Relerford 0-3, Bennett 4-7, Lee 1-1, B. Kalsow 0-1, Hicklin 0-1, Grusczynski 0-1). Total fouls: Lawrence 19, Stevens Point 18. Fouled out: none. Rebounds: Lawrence 24 (Braier 7), Stevens Point 28 (J. Kalsow 8). Turnovers: Lawrence 16, Stevens Point 8.

TOM CHARLESWORTH

TOM CHARLESWORTH

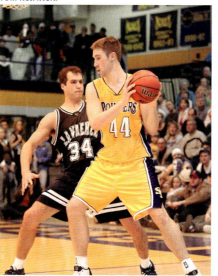

TOM KUJAWSKI

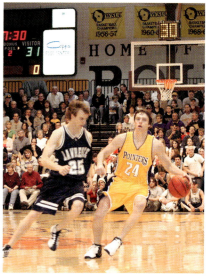

TOM CHARLESWORTH

TOM KUJAWSKI

TOM CHARLESWORTH

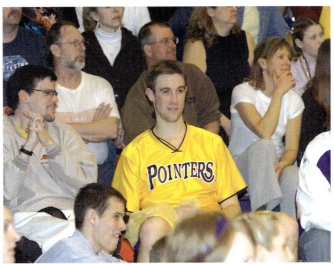

TOM KUJAWSKI

Above: A sold-out Quandt Fieldhouse

Below Left: Eric Maus maneuvers down low.

Below Right: Jason Kalsow and John Ringelstetter share a laugh towards the end of the Pionters 79-45 win over Lawrence

NCAA DIVISION III BASKETBALL TOURNAMENT

Pointers to host NCAA Sectional

Top: Pointer fans raise their special cheer cards provided by the Stevens Point Journal for the NCAA sectional games.

Bottom: Fans of all ages enjoyed cheering on the Pointers during the NCAA sectional.

By Scott Williams

Home sweet home.

The University of Wisconsin-Stevens Point men's basketball team will roll out the welcome mat to three guests this week. Four teams from across the country will compete at the Quandt Fieldhouse in Stevens Point for a spot in the NCAA Division III Final Four as the Pointers will host a sectional tournament Friday and Saturday.

UW-Stevens Point (25-3), ranked No. 1 in the most recent D3hoops.com poll, will host the University of Puget Sound of Tacoma, Wash. on Friday at 8 p.m. Hanover (Ind.) College meets Trinity (Texas) University in the first game at 6 p.m. The winners will play Saturday at 7 p.m.

The Pointers also played Puget Sound in last year's sectional semifinal and defeated the Loggers 100-79.

"Obviously we're thrilled," UWSP coach Jack Bennett said. "As everything broke down last night (Saturday) and we got the results from other games, we thought we felt like we had a legitimate shot to host."

It marks the first time UW-Stevens Point has hosted a men's sectional tournament. The Pointers are playing in their fourth sectional in nine years. They won last year's event in Tacoma, Wash. and lost title games in 2000 in Storm Lake, Iowa and 1997 in Lincoln, Neb.

The winner of the sectional will advance to Salem, Va. for the Final Four on March 18-19.

"I think the positives outweigh the perceived negatives," said Bennett of the potential distractions. "The fact is we play well on our home floor and I would much rather keep the routine the way it is with practice and classes."

DOUG WOJCIK

DOUG WOJCIK

NCAA DIVISION III BASKETBALL TOURNAMENT

Loyal fans make Point a great tourney site

By Scott Williams

Hundreds of University of Wisconsin-Stevens Point men's basketball fans woke at the crack of dawn Monday in hopes of getting a ticket to this weekend's NCAA tournament game.

In about two hours, the university's initial allotment of 1,200 tickets was gone.

Standing in line were a good number of UWSP students, but the vast majority were community members. Businessmen and women, stay-at-home mothers, lawyers, teachers, UWSP alum - they came from all walks of life.

The wide range of people focused on a common goal - scoring a ticket - is evidence of the tremendous impact UWSP has on central Wisconsin.

This weekend offers a historical moment for the Pointers. They'll host their first ever NCAA men's sectional tournament. The university also will host the NCAA Division III women's hockey quarterfinals this weekend, which, like the hoops sectional, has a berth in the Final Four at stake.

Stevens Point has proven itself as a host of choice. Much of that is due to the professional staff in the athletic department, media relations and administration that help to make the tournaments run so smoothly. And certainly UWSP has earned a reputation among its Division III peers for its quality athletic programs. But the NCAA has other interests as well, namely money.

Host an NCAA game in Stevens Point, and it will sell out. There's no doubt. Fans here are loyal - to more than the team - to the university as a whole.

It's easy to assume that such loyalty is the product of winning programs. But we remember years when the teams weren't going quite so well. Still, the stands were packed. The university has woven itself into the fabric of the community. And we reap the benefits.

Area hotel rooms are packed to the brim this weekend as four Division III teams go up against the Pointers in both hockey and basketball. The restaurants will benefit from increased traffic, as will gas stations, grocery stores and entertainment venues.

Average community members aren't as interested in the revenue generated through room taxes or profits by area businesses. It's hard to wrap your mind around the residual benefits that affect their daily lives. All they know is that the University of Wisconsin-Stevens Point is an intricate part of their lives. Tickets might be hard to come by this weekend, but there's always next year. We promise you won't be disappointed.

Bottom: Fans waited in line for up to two hours for a chance to purchase tickets to the Pointers playoff games.

TOM KUJAWSKI

NCAA DIVISION III
BASKETBALL TOURNAMENT

Pointers' offense fights on without its head

By Scott Williams

Top: Tamaris Relerford breaks the Lawrence pressure.

Bottom: Redshirt-freshman Steve Hicklin will handle the point guard position for the injured Tamaris Relerford.

It's arguably the most important position in men's college basketball. Take the starting point guard out of the lineup and it's like cutting off the team's head, and possibly an arm.

Need proof? See Marquette University without Travis Diener.

That torso you'll see running around at Quandt Fieldhouse during its Sweet 16 game tonight is the University of Wisconsin-Stevens Point men's team. Senior point guard Tamaris Relerford suffered a broken hand during the Pointers' 79-45 second round win over Lawrence Universirty last Saturday.

There is never a good time for a season-ending injury. But the NCAA Division III Tournament would have to rank as one of the more unfortunate. The timing doesn't give Pointer coach Jack Bennett or his players much time to adjust to life without Relerford.

Relerford now has to adjust with life without basketball as he closes out his college basketball career in street clothes sitting next to his coaches. Four years of practices and hard work will come to an anti-climatic conclusion for the Beloit native. Relerford can take some consolation from knowing that no one can take the championship ring he owns, or the memories of that magical 2003-04 season away from him.

There is no denying the top-ranked and defending national champion Pointers will miss Relerford's ball-handling expertise and experience running the offense to some extent. He started 44 games over the past two seasons, and during that time demonstrated an uncanny knack for knocking down big shots at important times.

His contributions and meaning to the team runs much deeper, however. It may be next to impossible to make up for Relerford's tenacious on-the-ball defense and lightning-quick ability to jump into passing lanes.

Fortunately for the Pointers, the cupboard of point guards at UWSP is hardly empty. Bennett has a number of options to choose from as the Pointers prepare for tonight's game against the University of Puget Sound (Wash.).

The leading candidate to move into the starting point guard role is freshman red-shirt Steve Hicklin. The list also includes freshman Shawn Lee and senior Kyle Grusczynski. Even 6-foot-7 power forward Jason Kalsow, the school's all-time career scoring leader, is comfortable bringing the basketball up court.

Coincidentally, Hicklin moved into the role as the primary back-up to Relerford after Lee suffered a broken hand earlier in the season. All three have seen considerable time at the point position during the course of the season, and received important minutes during the second half against Lawrence. The trio combined for 12 points, six assists and not a single turnover over the final 20 minutes.

But the Vikings presented nothing that closely resembles the helter-skelter 94-foot pressure Puget Sound will throw at UWSP tonight. The Loggers are relentless in their desire to force turnovers and create steals.

Always a point of emphasis in the UWSP program, taking care of the basketball will take on extra importance tonight without Relerford around to serve as a one-man press breaker.

In the end, the Pointers may consider themselves lucky to have a four-headed monster when it comes to the all-important position of point guard. Only time will tell if it's enough.

TOM CHARLESWORTH

TOM KUJAWSKI

NCAA DIVISION III
BASKETBALL TOURNAMENT

Pointer tickets go quickly

By Scott Williams

TOM KUJAWSKI

Above: Lucas Elliott purchases tickets for the Pointers playoff game from Chris Seefeldt at the University Ticket Center.

"Maybe I'll get in line again Friday at 6 o'clock and take a day of vacation. I thought I'd be in line for 15 or 20 minutes. Once you're in line, you don't want to get out."

—Pointer fan Steve Bandy

The bandwagon is getting crowded for the University of Wisconsin-Stevens Point men's basketball team.

Die-hard fans and those who have recently caught Pointer fever were lined up when doors opened at the UWSP box office in the University Center on Monday morning.

In less than three hours, the school's 1,200-ticket allotment for Friday's NCAA Division III sectional semifinal game at the Quandt Fieldhouse was sold out.

"Based on the (Wisconsin Intercollegiate Athletic Conference) tournament and the first round of the NCAAs, we knew the demand would be great," UWSP Athletic Director Frank O'Brien said. "Unfortunately, we're only allotted a certain amount of tickets."

For those fans who don't have a ticket in their hands or the mail, all is not lost. The three visiting schools - University of Puget Sound (Wash.), Trinity (Texas) University and Hanover (Ind.) College - each receive 400 tickets. The deadline for ticket sales is noon Thursday.

"I have to make sure I know exactly where I am and what I have. I need to know what I'm talking about and exactly what will be available," said UWSP box office manager Chris Seefeldt of the possibility of returned tickets from the other three schools.

More than 300 people were standing in line when the box office opened its doors Monday. Steve Bandy was one of them. After about two hours of waiting, the Pointer alum heard the dreaded words, "We're sold out." He figures he was seven or eight people away from purchasing his tickets.

"It was very frustrating, especially when you heard rumors they didn't put a cap on the number of tickets people could buy," Bandy said. "This is the first time ever I didn't have tickets for a game of this magnitude."

Despite his frustration, he intends to be back Friday if tickets become available.

"Maybe I'll get in line again Friday at 6 o'clock and take a day of vacation," Bandy said. "I thought I'd be in line for 15 or 20 minutes. Once you're in line, you don't want to get out."

The rush for tickets didn't surprise Seefeldt. She credited her employees with keeping things in order Monday morning.

"I can't say enough about my girls. They've been wonderful and have done over and above what I should expect. They really stepped up to the plate," Seefeldt said.

Locating tickets isn't the only problem the athletic department has encountered.

As the host school for NCAA men's basketball and women's hockey tournament games this weekend, UWSP is responsible for staffing each event.

"It has been a lot of work, but it's definitely a fun problem to have," UWSP assistant athletics director and Sports Information Director Jim Strick said.

"It's very similar to last season when we had three teams in the Final Four. But it's a lot different in that both events are at home this year."

NCAA DIVISION III
BASKETBALL TOURNAMENT

FOR THE LOVE OF THE TEAM
Only the lucky score tickets to Pointers game

By Alex Shaine

A University of Wisconsin-Stevens Point janitor reported something, well, suspicious when he was cleaning the University Center late Thursday night - two young men wearing fur hats that were camped out next to the campus Box Office.

The oddly dressed duo - later determined to be UWSP freshmen Matt Oehmichen and Mike Bolinski - spent the night outside the Box Office to have the first crack at tickets for the Pointer men's basketball team's Sweet 16 game in the NCAA tournament. They were among the hundreds of fans who were denied tickets when the first round of tickets sold out on Monday.

"I was angry (on Monday)," Bolinski said, "and I wanted to make sure I got tickets this time."

Oehmichen and Bolinski got their wish. They were the first to purchase passes for Friday's game when the ticket counter opened at 9 a.m. But about a third of the 200 fans who lined up early Friday morning for tickets weren't so fortunate. The remaining 600 tickets for Friday's game sold out in a mere 43 minutes.

A crowd of about 60 ticketless fans let loose a collective groan when a voice bellowed through the room telling the eager crowd, "I'm sorry, but tickets are sold out."

For Chester Przybylski of Stevens Point, this meant having to break the news to his young son, who had been looking forward to attending the game with his father.

"I'm awestruck," Przybylski said. "More for my little guy because he wanted to watch."

UWSP junior Kelly Thoma was next in line when the announcement came.

"We were here on Monday for two hours and here for four hours this morning ... This is pretty upsetting," Thoma said.

University ticket-sellers tried to spread the tickets around by limiting ticket sales to a maximum of four per person. But a steady flow of callers purchased hundreds of tickets over the phone. Some of those who showed up in person to buy tickets were able to do so by picking up the nearest phone.

"I heard that they were taking phone orders, so I walked over there and called from a campus phone," said UWSP Junior Paul Logan, pointing to a house phone at the other end of the waiting room.

With a combined 1,800 tickets sold on Monday and Friday, the university's box office sold just about all of its tickets for Friday's game. The university reserves a couple hundred seats in Quandt Field House for band members and people who travel with each team, according to Box Office Manager Chris Seefeldt.

TOM KUJAWSKI

Top: UWSP freshmen Matt Oehmichen and Mike Bolinski spent the night outside the UWSP Box Office to make sure they were first in line for Pointer tickets.

Bottom: A young UWSP fan reminds the Pointers of what they have to do against Puget Sound.

DOUG WOJCIK

NCAA DIVISION III
BASKETBALL TOURNAMENT

POINTERS WORK ON MIND GAME
Bennett teaches, learns from 'students'

By Scott Williams

Left: Head Coach Jack Bennett holds a classroom session for his team prior to the NCAA Sweet 16.

DOUG WOJCIK

Professor Jack Bennett stands next to a hi-tech video machine at the front of the class.

His students - a.k.a. the University of Wisconsin-Stevens Point men's basketball team - don't dare entertain thoughts of shooting spit-balls.

Class is in session and the lesson on this day is avoiding a similar letdown in the second half against the University of Puget Sound (Wash.) this year, as was the case for the Pointers in the Sweet 16 of last year's tournament.

Not all the teaching is done on the basketball court.

"It's a lot easier to see some of the things the coaches are talking about on a screen, than trying to describe it in practice," UWSP junior forward Mike Prey said.

Several days a week, the Pointers men's basketball team heads to Room 146 in the Quandt Fieldhouse before practice. A classroom session can last anywhere from 15 to 20 minutes. Then there are days where the study hall lasts 45 minutes or an hour.

"I think we've been in here three or four years. It's become one of the great teaching stations," Bennett said. "This room has become a very big part of our teaching."

Only so much teaching can take place on the basketball floor. Plus, at this time of the season the redundancy of running the same offenses and defenses day after day can become monotonous. The classroom has all the latest in hi-tech amenities, including a video machine that can project notes Bennett has taken after games, without the need for transparencies, or videotapes. As if that wasn't enough help, a whiteboard also provides yet another teaching tool.

During much of the day, the room is home to health, exercise science and athletics classes for the rest of the student body. "With the modern age of players this group responds better to visual stuff. You can't just say stuff anymore. You have to show players," Bennett said. "It gives us a nice balance between the mental part of the game and physical repetition."

Unlike some basketball programs, Bennett doesn't make notebooks mandatory for the players. Not only does such a casual approach prevent spit-balls, but it makes the classroom portion of practice unlike attending regular classes.

In addition, Bennett doesn't believe in leading a dictatorship or being a taskmaster. He welcomes input from the assistant coaches and players.

"I think coaches learn as they go along that players have some of the best ideas. They've been out there and through the battles," Bennett said. "I listen to all of them but ultimately I make the final call."

The lesson on Tuesday was making sure the Pointers maintain their intensity for the entire 40 minutes, and finish any easy scoring chances that may arise in their Sweet 16 game with the Loggers. Last year, UWSP took a 50-30 lead at halftime only to see Puget Sound eventually close the deficit to seven points. Missed lay-ups and a drop-off in intensity by UWSP helped the Loggers out.

After spending most of the week attending classes, another couple hours in a classroom setting as part of basketball practice can wear a little thin on students. Players point out the coaches do a good job of getting the information across without becoming overbearing or tedious.

"You have to do stuff like this because this is a game of learning," Prey said. "It's the same in this classroom, just like everything else with school."

FEATURE
UWSP ASSISTANTS

Bennett leans heavily on UWSP Assistants

Top: Assistant Coach Aaron Bonnett.

Below: Associate Head Coach Bob Semling.

By Scott Williams

Bob Semling sits in his cramped office looking at tapes of upcoming opponents. An associate coach for the University of Wisconsin-Stevens Point men's basketball team, Semling will spend hours splicing together a scouting report on York (Pa.) - the Pointers' semifinal opponent in the NCAA Division III Final Four on Friday.

It all comes with the job, says Semling, who is in his second stint as an assistant with the Pointers.

"My responsibilities include scouting and game preparation. I'll study an opponent and look for tendencies and little things that might help make a difference," said Semling, a native of Merrill. "I also work with player development. I'll take one or two players and really work with them one-on-one and help them improve their games. Plus, I work the basketball camps and do some recruiting."

Tucked away in another corner of the office is assistant Aaron Bonnett. In his fourth year on the Pointers staff, Bonnett is busy searching for information on the boys teams at the WIAA State Tournament. Bonnett is searching high and low for any possible future Pointers. Recruiting is a year-round job and has Bonnett living on the road for much of the basketball season.

"Any night we're not playing, I'm on the road recruiting. There are a lot of late nights when I come rolling in around midnight or 1 a.m. I love the recruiting part," Bonnett said. "It's a huge responsibility to see recruits and evaluate the type of players we want here at Point. I know what kind of kids coach Bennett likes and who fit the coach's system. But I'm not all about the glory. I'll grab a broom and sweep the floor if they need me to. I'll do whatever they need."

The primary beneficiaries of all the hard work and long hours Bonnett and Semling put in are the players. Coming in a close second is Pointers coach Jack Bennett. With Semling and Bonnett taking care of much of the administrative and scouting aspects of coaching, Bennett can concentrate on fine-tuning his offensive and defensive systems. He can also focus on motivating and maintaining a healthy team philosophy.

"They do set the table for me, I can't deny. Those guys really are my right-hand men. Without them, I would be stretched more thin," Bennett said. "I have some truly unselfish assistants. For us, the whole is greater than the sum of the parts."

Bennett takes pride in not running a dictatorship with the Pointers. Though he seeks and accepts input and suggestions from his assistants, ultimately the final decision is Bennett's to make.

"We believe in one another. Whether they believe it or not, Bob and Aaron get a lot more input and freedom to be who they are than some coaching stops I've made," Bennett said. "I give them the latitude to know we're all in this together.

"One of the things I've learned if you're going to make a run at the national level is that you must base relationships with players and coaches on discipline and toughness with equal amounts of love and trust."

Bennett has a special bond with Semling. The pair crossed paths when Semling was a sophomore in high school. He was a counselor at a Milwaukee Bucks camp that Bennett was working while the coach at Marinette High School.

Bennett and Semling immediately hit it off on and off the court, with Bennett eventually asking Semling to join him on his staff at Wisconsin Rapids Lincoln. Semling eventually landed on the Pointers' staff in 1988.

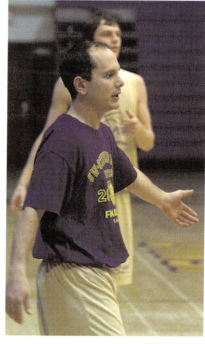
DOUG WOJCIK

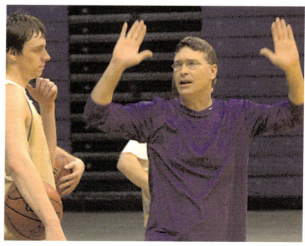
DOUG WOJCIK

Above: Bonnett and Semling follow the action during the NCAA Final Four.

TOM CHARLESWORTH

"We kind of clicked and stayed in touch. We reconnected even before we were together at Rapids. We obviously know each other well. I really think we're colleagues and friends first," Semling said.

After graduating from Ripon College, Bonnett served an apprenticeship for three years at his high school alma mater Adams-Friendship under coach Steve Klaas before joining the UWSP staff. The past four years have opened Bonnett's eyes to what being a college basketball coach, and one at a premier Division III school, all entails.

"I'm learning all the time. I'm grateful and so happy to be in a position to see first-hand the way coach Bennett can motivate and teach players," Bonnett said. "I can't replace this experience. I feel fortunate and blessed to have a chance to work under coach Bennett."

Semling eventually left the Pointers in 1995 to scratch an itch for Division I basketball. He accepted an assistant job under Mike Heideman at UW-Green Bay. A new athletic director came in and decided to make a coaching change after seven seasons with the Phoenix. After a one-year stay at the University of New Mexico as the director of basketball operations, Semling returned to his roots.

"When Kenny Koelbl left, I got a lot of calls from some great potential candidates to fill the position. But I focused on Bob. I wanted to have someone I could trust and who knew the ropes. He has a lot of experience," Bennett said. "I sure can't ask for two greater assistant coaches."

Semling was in the running for several Division III coaching jobs when he went to Green Bay, and still has aspirations of becoming a college coach at some level in the future. For now he is content to enjoy the ride and help one of the top Division III programs in the country.

"Jack called me and said I might have a position open. Maybe there was a reason for that," Semling said. "At this stage of my career this was the best decision for my family.

"First and foremost I wanted my three kids to be in central Wisconsin for their high school years. I really wanted them to be near their grandpas and grandmas, and enjoy those years."

Coach Aaron Bonnett has a nice ring to it, but he plans to put off any such career advancement for a period of time yet. He relishes the opportunity to learn under Bennett and absorb everything he can.

"All the great coaches have some things in common and it's great to be able to see what makes them so special," Bonnett said. "I'm just taking it all in and learning how I'm going to use it when I'm coaching."

NCAA DIVISION III SECTIONALS

UWSP rolls into Elite Eight

By Scott Williams

University of Wisconsin-Stevens Point men's basketball coach Jack Bennett likes to refer to it as a "kamikaze" defense. The only problem is trying to figure out if he's talking about the University of Puget Sound or his team Friday night.

Either way, the Pointers continued to be the death of the Loggers in the Sweet 16 of the NCAA Division III tournament. The top-ranked and defending champion Pointers held Puget Sound 30 points below its season scoring average and rolled to an 81-63 victory before a full house at the Quandt Fieldhouse.

"One of the keys tonight is we held them to 63 points," Bennett said. "As usual, this was a hard-fought physical battle. The game can get a little ragged, but not because effort is lacking."

The Loggers, ranked seventh in the latest D3hoops.com poll, finished 22-4.

For a brief moment, their season looked like it might be over at halftime as Stevens Point built a 20-point lead with less than 2 minutes left. Puget Sound never pushed the panic button.

"This was a great environment. We played a great team and didn't quite get it done," Loggers coach Eric Bridgeland said.

Not before giving the defending national champions a scare in the second half.

Puget Sound finally found a hole in the Pointers' 3-2 zone and 6-foot-6 center Zack McVey kept ripping it bigger and bigger. McVey scored eight of his team-high 19 points in the first 7 minutes of the half, as the Loggers closed the gap to 53-45.

"Stevens Point does a pretty good job of making it tough to get the ball in there," Bridgeland said. "Zack is what got us here. I never in my wildest dreams thought this team would get to this point."

Just as the collar was starting to tighten, Bennett made a game-changing adjustment on defense. That was when the Pointers switched to a 1-3-1 zone, and Puget Sound watched its offense come to a standstill.

"Surprise, surprise with the 1-3-1," Bennett said. "I keep saying I'm not married to any one defense. I'm wedded to any defense that gives us a chance to win."

Top: The Pointer faithful cheer on their home team.

Below: Kyle Grusczynski drills a three-pointer early on against Puget Sound.

DOUG WOJCIK

DOUG WOJCIK

DOUG WOJCIK

Above: *Head Coach Jack Bennett gives his players instruction during a timeout against Puget Sound.*

And the Loggers were unable to rely on their defense to make up for the problems on the other end.

Pointer freshman guard Steve Hicklin, making his first career start, and Jason Kalsow refused to let relentless pressure do any serious damage. Hicklin, stepping into the shoes of injured Tamaris Relerford, played like a seasoned veteran. He finished with 15 points, three assists and two turnovers.

"I was a little nervous to make my first start in a Sweet 16 game. But Tamaris remembered what worked last year, so I wasn't out there by myself," Hicklin said.

Kalsow overcame early foul trouble to score 16 points and hand out seven assists in a performance that resulted in Bridgeland calling him "the white Magic Johnson."

Just another typical game for the player of the year candidate.

"Kalsow is a trump card for us. At 6-7, he can step out and give us some relief at the point guard spot. That is why I keep saying he is the most complete player at this level," Bennett said. "The guys listened to me a little bit. I told them we had to have 14 or less turnovers."

The Loggers, who forced exactly 14 turnovers, geared their defense to stopping Nick Bennett in the first half. That left the door open for Eric Maus and Hicklin to ransack the cutting lanes. Maus tied a career high with 18 points.

Bennett eventually found a way to get his points - namely at the free-throw line. He finished with a game-high 22 points, including a 9-for-11 effort at the line.

Stevens Point went 28 for 32 at the line while the Loggers were 12 for 14.

"The length of Stevens Point is not something you're use to and we don't see the 1-3-1 zone often. Put those together and it's difficult to know what should be done," Bridgeland said.

Left to Right:

- *Nick Bennett soars to block the shot of Puget Sound player Ryan DeLong.*
- *Jon Krull, Nick Bennett and Eric Maus apply the defensive pressure.*
- *Pointer ballboy, D.J. Loken, keeps the court dry.*
- *Gbenga Awe goes up high to block a shot.*

POINTERS 81, LOGGERS 63

PUGET SOUND (63) - Zack McVey 6-11 7-8 19, Chas Curtiss 6-15 1-2 17, Chris O'Donnell 3-5 0-0 6, Jeremy Cross 2-7 2-2 7, Josh Walker 2-5 0-0 4, Taylor Marsh 0-2 0-0 0, Aubrey Shelton 2-6 2-2 7, Jordan Beede 1-2 0-0 3, Ryan DeLong 0-2 0-0 0, Weston Wood 0-1 0-0 0. Totals 22-56 12-14 63.

UW-STEVENS POINT (81) - Jon Krull 2-3 0-2 4, Jason Kalsow 6-7 4-4 16, Eric Maus 7-7 4-4 18, Steve Hicklin 3-7 9-9 15, Nick Bennett 5-10 9-11 22, Kyle Grusczynski 1-5 2-2 4, Brian Bauer 1-4 0-0 2. Totals 25-43 28-32 81.

University of Puget Sound	23	40	- 63
UW-Stevens Point	39	42	- 81

3-point goals: Puget Sound 7-26 (Curtiss 4-12, Cross 1-5, Walker 0-3, Marsh 0-2, Shelton 1-2, Beede 1-1, DeLong 0-1), Stevens Point 3-11 (Hicklin 0-4, Bennett 3-4, Grusczynski 0-3). Total fouls: Puget Sound 25, Stevens Point 14. Fouled out: Curtiss, Walker. Technical fouls: Coach Bennett. Rebounds: Puget Sound 22 (O'Donnell 7), Stevens Point 33 (J. Kalsow, Maus 7). Turnovers: Puget Sound 11, Stevens Point 11. Att. - 2,746.

DOUG WOJCIK

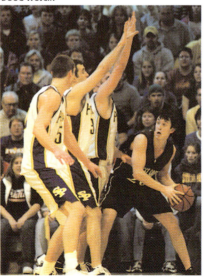
DOUG WOJCIK

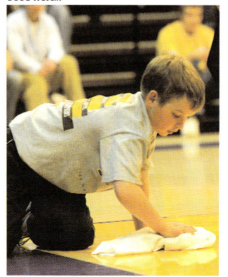
DOUG WOJCIK

DOUG WOJCIK

Top Left: Jason Kalsow slams one home against Puget Sound.

Top Right: Brian Bauer blocks the shot of Puget Sound center Zack McVey.

DOUG WOJCIK

Bottom Right: A sold-out Quandt Fieldhouse.

DOUG WOJCIK

NCAA DIVISION III SECTIONALS
Back to Salem

Top: The opening tip.

Bottom: Jason Kalsow finds it tough going down low early on against the Tigers of Trinity.

DOUG WOJCIK

By Scott Williams

STEVENS POINT - There is nothing quite like the late winter vacation hot spot of Salem, Va. for spring break.

The University of Wisconsin-Stevens Point men's basketball team had so much fun last year, it couldn't resist a return trip. The Pointers are heading to the NCAA Division III Final Four for a second straight year.

Surviving an intense pressure cooker and taking the best shots Trinity (Texas) University could throw, the Pointers emerged with a 61-55 win in an Elite Eight thriller at the Quandt Fieldhouse on Saturday night.

"It even feels better this time around. To be able to share it with our family and these great fans is special," UWSP coach Jack Bennett said. "That was the true definition of the term 'gut-check.' I can't say enough about the ability to execute under pressure and the courage of this team," he added.

The top-ranked Pointers (27-3) will face York (Pa.) in the national semifinal on Friday at 7 p.m. (CST) in Salem. Calvin (Mich.) and Rochester (N.Y.) will meet in the other semifinal.

In front of a delirious home crowd - and with the legacy of a superlative senior class on the line - the Pointers dug deep.

Trinity didn't collapse down the stretch or cave in under the wild environment. This was a game the Pointers won. The defending national champions ultimately prevailed because of their uncanny ability to make big plays at critical times.

"You have to give that team lots of credit. They did what they had to win the game,"

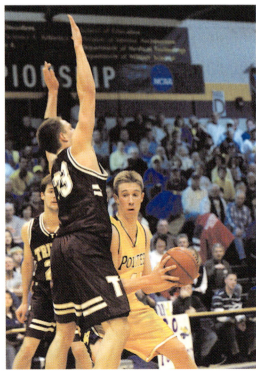

DOUG WOJCIK

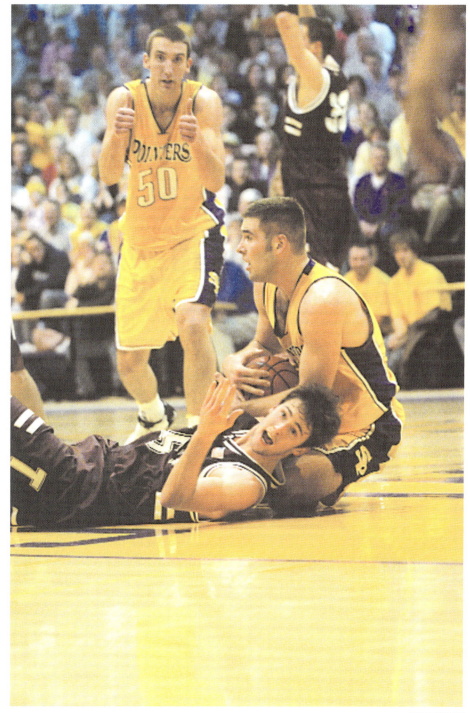

Left: Jon Krull ties up a Trinity player for a jump ball as teammate Eric Maus makes the call.

Right: Injured senior point guard Tamaris Relerford watches the action from the Pointer bench.

DOUG WOJCIK

Trinity senior guard Jason Morris said. "They made plays on defense and earned it."

Kyle Grusczynski created a running shot in the lane to give UWSP the lead for good at 52-50 with 2:28 left in regulation. Jason Kalsow, who saw his streak of 63 straight games in double figures snapped, contributed with a huge block. Eric Maus grabbed several key defensive rebounds and Jon Krull provided a monumental 3-point play off an offensive rebound.
"We're all making plays for one another and don't want to give up on one another," Nick Bennett said.

And let's not forget about sectional tournament most valuable player Nick Bennett. The senior guard created a crucial 3-point play with 1:31 showing on the clock and drained four straight free throws down the stretch.

He finished with a game-high 28 points, including 5 of 11 shooting from 3-point range.

DOUG WOJCIK

"Bennett and Kalsow are really hard to guard," Trinity coach Pat Cunningham said. "Bennett hit a couple threes early. He knocked the dog-gone things in and made shots."

Trinity had the Pointers on the ropes in the second half, with much of the credit going to Morris, who did his best to quiet a raucous crowd.

"I like to play in front of a big crowd. I use their energy and pretend they're cheering for me," said Morris, whose team played at

POINTERS 61, TIGERS 55

TRINITY UNIVERSITY (55) - Peter Murray 4-8 2-2 12, Andy Bates 1-7 2-2 4, Sean Devins 2-9 2-4 6, Jason Morris 7-16 4-5 20, Chad Stroberg 3-4 0-0 9, Ross Burt 1-4 0-0 2, Mitch Walker 0-2 0-0 0, James Lake 1-3 0-0 2. Totals 19-53 10-13 55.

UW-STEVENS POINT (61) - Jon Krull 2-4 2-3 6, Jason Kalsow 4-13 0-0 8, Eric Maus 4-8 0-0 8, Steve Hicklin 1-1 1-1 3, Nick Bennett 9-19 5-5 28, Kyle Grusczynski 3-5 2-2 8, Brian Bauer 0-1 0-0 0. Totals 23-51 10-11 61.

Trinity University	24	31	- 55
UW-Stevens Point	28	33	- 61

3-point goals: Trinity 7-23 (Murray 2-3, Bates 0-2, Morris 2-7, Stroberg 3-4, Burt 0-3, Walker 0-2, Lake 0-2), Stevens Point (Krull 0-1, Kalsow 0-3, Bennett 5-11, Grusczynski 0-1). Total fouls: Trinity 16, Stevens Point 16. Fouled out: Stroberg. Rebounds: Trinity 35 (Devins 10), Stevens Point 30 (Kalsow 10). Turnovers: Trinity 15, Stevens Point 11. Att. - 2,720.

DOUG WOJCIK

Left to Right:
- Coach Bennett shares his displeasure in a call as the official runs by.
- Head Coach Jack Bennett gets his point across to Kyle Grusczynski during a Pointer timeout.
- Eric Maus with the jump hook for two.
- Trinity's Sean Devins shoots a jumper over Jason Kalsow.

DOUG WOJCIK   DOUG WOJCIK   DOUG WOJCIK

Left: Kyle Grusczynski challenges a three-pointer by Trinity guard Jason Morris that would have tied the game with time winding down.

DOUG WOJCIK

DOUG WOJCIK

Above: *Jon Krull and Kyle Grusczynski double check on what the coaching staff wants late in the Pointers 61-55 win over Trinity.*

Left: *The Pointer bench senses a victory.*

DOUG WOJCIK

Division I Texas A & M earlier in the season. "This is the craziest crowd I've played against."

Utilizing his quickness to create open space for himself, Morris scored nine points in the first 5 minutes as the Tigers (23-7) erased a 28-24 deficit at halftime. He finished with a team-high 20 points - 15 coming in the second half. Trinity capitalized on his hot hand to grab a 49-48 lead with 3:34 left.

Trinity's Sean Devins, a 6-foot-10 center, didn't hurt the Pointers with points. But his intimidating presence in the paint made it nearly impossible for any of UWSP's interior players, especially Kalsow.

"That team (Trinity) was as good as any Final Four teams we'll see," coach Bennett said. "You can't be this good under pressure unless you've been under the fire before."

Just when things were starting to look grim, the Pointers reached down for every memory from their big-game experience over the past three years. As a result, UWSP kept its dream of back-to-back national titles alive.

"My dad and I talked about how we wanted to get this team to this type of level. The past three years this team has been one of the top teams in the nation, and that has been special," Nick Bennett said.

Above: *Jason Kalsow blocks a Trinity shot with :16 seconds left to seal the victory for the Pointers.*

Below: *The Pointers celebrate their return to the Final Four.*

DOUG WOJCIK

DOUG WOJCIK

DOUG WOJCIK

Top Left: Seniors John Gleich and Nick Bennett share a victory hug.

Top Right: Head Coach Jack Bennett cuts down the nets after a hard-fought win over Trinity.

Bottom Left: The Pointers huddle up after disposing of Trinity as the television cameras try to get a shot.

NCAA DIVISION III
MEN'S FINAL FOUR

Pointers lead lands on rookie Hicklin

By Scott Williams

DOUG WOJCIK

Above: Redshirt-freshman Steve Hicklin has performed like a veteran.

SALEM, Va. - Steve Hicklin is a patient man.

The red-shirt freshman point guard on the University of Wisconsin-Stevens Point men's basketball team figured his chance to see extensive playing time - and possibly start - wouldn't come until next season. That timetable was sped up by about eight months when Hicklin made his first collegiate start against the University of Puget Sound (Wash.) in Friday's sectional semifinal of the NCAA Division III tournament.

"I tried not to think about it a lot," Hicklin said. "I was a little nervous. I was making my first start in the Sweet 16."

Injuries to Tamaris Relerford and Shawn Lee have thrust the Sussex native into a featured role as the Pointers vie for back-to-back national championships. A couple months earlier and the responsibility of being the starting point guard in all likelihood would have fallen on the slightly less broad shoulders of Lee.

Lee, a Marshfield Columbus product who attended UW-Marshfield in 2003-04, opened the season as the primary backup to Relerford. But a broken hand suffered in practice sidelined Lee for four weeks.

"I thought I was playing well and getting a decent amount of minutes at the time," Lee said. "I'm just going to do the best I can with whatever minutes I get. If that means 2 or 3 minutes to give a guy a break, then that's fine. That is the thing about having such a good program. We have so many different options."

When opportunity came calling, Hicklin performed like a seasoned veteran. Faced with the unenviable task of dealing with the Loggers' non-stop, length-of-the-court harassment, Hicklin chalked up a career-high 15 points, three assists and only a pair of turnovers.

"When his number was called, he stepped up. Steve didn't get to ease into the water, he had to dive right in," UWSP coach Jack Bennett said.

According to Hicklin, the helter-skelter approach by Puget Sound on defense might have made his job a little easier.

"It's a lot different than what we usually see, but it was easier in that you had two guys on you, so you just had to make sure to make the obvious pass," he said.

In addition to handling the Loggers pressure, Hicklin led the team in minutes played that game. He was solid enough to get another start against Trinity (Texas) University in an Elite Eight game the next night. Odds are Hicklin will hear his name called again when the Pointers starting lineup is announced for their national semifinal game with York (Pa.) at the Salem Civic Center on Friday at 7 p.m.

"What that tells me is that he was playing pretty well," Bennett said after he was informed about how much playing time Hicklin got in the Sweet 16. "What it did was get Steve some action in a pressure situation."

With the likes of Jason Kalsow and Nick Bennett around, there is no pressure on Hicklin to carry the offense. On top of this, Lee and senior Kyle Grusczynski are also capable of handling the point guard duties in case of foul trouble or matchup problems.

Hicklin has been able to shine under the newly-revamped red-shirt program available to Division III student-athletes, allowing players to practice with their team without losing a year of athletic eligibility.

The practice has been eliminated by the NCAA at the Division III level at the prodding and urging of private schools who see red-shirting as an unfair edge for public universities.

"Steve is a product of red-shirting," Bennett said. "He got a chance to practice with us last season and I think that helped him."

Losing a starting point guard might be death wish for a lot of college basketball teams. But the defending national champions have the depth at the position to overcome the loss of Relerford at the most important time of the season.

"I'm really proud of our program and team to absorb this kind of heavy hit at such a crucial time of the season," Bennett said. "The guys have picked it up a lot. This could've been a devastating situation."

NCAA DIVISION III
MEN'S FINAL FOUR

Center: Billboards around town promoted the upcoming NCAA Final Four.

Bottom: The Salem Civic Center concourse.

Ready for tip-off

By Scott Williams

SALEM, Va. - To hear York College men's basketball coach Jeff Gamber talk, one wonders why the Spartans even made the journey from the rolling hills of south-central Pennsylvania.

Gamber gives the impression York (28-2) will be thoroughly outclassed and overmatched in its NCAA Division III national semifinal with the University of Wisconsin-Stevens Point tonight.

"They are an outstanding team," Gamber said of the Pointers. "Flat out, we have to be terrific to have a chance. People ask me what weaknesses Stevens Point has. I haven't found one. We haven't played against a team like Stevens Point this season."

Pointers coach Jack Bennett isn't buying what Gamber is trying to sell.

"That's a veteran coach trying to set us up," said Bennett, whose team is trying to become the first Division III school to win back-to-back national titles since UW-Platteville in 1998-99. "They're a rugged team with veteran players."

The Spartans, ranked No. 19 in the most recent D3hoops.com poll, enter the game with an impressive list of credentials. The Capital Athletic Conference champions bring a 14-game winning streak into the Final Four, including a 70-58 win over King's (Pa.) in the championship game of the Mahwah (N.J.) sectional.

"We didn't think about the NCAA tournament until we won the conference championship," said Gamber, who owns a 371-355 record in 28 seasons. "It was never on the radar screen. In college basketball, you'd better be playing pretty good in the month of February."

The top-ranked Pointers won't have to look far to find a couple pretty good York players.

Junior Brandon Bushey, a 6-foot-3 guard, leads four players averaging in double figures with 16.5 points a game. He was named the conference and sectional MVP.

Chad McGowan was selected the CAC freshman of the year and ranks fourth on the team in scoring at 10.4. York averages 80.9 points a game and is 15th in the country in 3-point field-goal percentage (40.3).

"The competition isn't going to be any easier this year," Pointer junior forward/center Brian Bauer said. "They're obviously a good team or they wouldn't be here. They have size and they're a good rebounding team. We're going to have to be ready."

UWSP has something to counteract the Spartans' proficiency from behind the arc - it's called defense. The Pointers (27-3) are ranked second in the country, allowing only 56.2 points a game. They showed off their stingy nature in the Sweet 16 when they held the University of Puget Sound to 63 points - 30 below its average.

Bauer figures there is no reason to change what has gotten the team this far.

"We've been defending people well all season," said Bauer, an Auburndale native. "We can outscore people if we have to, but we want to play solid 'D' and have our offense complement our defense."

Bennett likes the business-like approach his team has taken during its return trip to the Final Four. There has been no hint of overconfidence or complacency.

"I see the right amount of focus with the right amount of assertiveness," Bennett said. "I get the feeling they're here to get something done, but while they're here they want to enjoy the trip."

York and the Pointers have one common opponent.

Both have played Edgewood College on its home court, with the Spartans earning an 80-77 victory on January 8, and UWSP picking up a 79-49 win January 20. But Bennett is quick to suggest nothing should be read into those results, or the fact the Pointers have previous Final Four experience.

Bennett expects things to be just as tough the second time around.

"All I know is you're going to be challenged and you have to meet that challenge," he said. "There will be a mighty struggle. You're going to have to sacrifice for your teammates. Then hopefully, you reach for the glory."

Below Left: The Pointers go through a workout in the Salem Civic Center.

TOM CHARLESWORTH

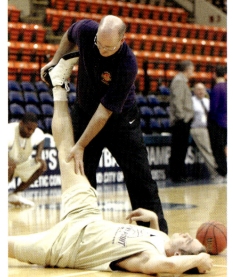

TOM CHARLESWORTH TOM CHARLESWORTH

Top Left: Assistant coach Jim Warzinik helps stretch out Jason Kalsow prior to practice.

Top Right: The Pointers scrimmage during a Final Four practice.

Below Right: Coach Bennett works on his jump shot. Pointer fans everywhere are thankful he didn't pass his shooting ability on to his son Nick!

TOM CHARLESWORTH

NCAA DIVISION III
MEN'S FINAL FOUR

POINTERS RECEIVE WARM WELCOME
Host family in Virginia treats basketball team to Southern hospitality

By Scott Williams

Below: Roger and Bonnie Surber

TOM CHARLESWORTH

SALEM, Va. - Roger and Bonnie Surber were thinking about adoption. When the couple finally made the decision to move forward, they did so in a Swiss Family Robinson sort of way.

Two years ago, the Surbers adopted the University of Wisconsin-Stevens Point men's basketball team. The Salem, Va., couple serves as a host family each year for the West sectional representative in the NCAA Division III Tournament since 1996.

No group of players have touched their lives quite like the Pointers.

"The kids are so much more open, so we've developed quite a relationship with them," said Bonnie, attired in a purple dress coat. "It's been so much more personal with them than the other teams. They're one of ours."

The feeling is mutual.

"They make us feel like family," Pointers junior forward Mike Prey said.

No one from Salem will be cheering louder for the Pointers in tonight's semifinal game with York (Pa.) than the Surbers. The players and coaches left an indelible impression on Bonnie and Roger, the sheriff of Salem.

UWSP coach Jack Bennett says the coaching staff and his players are the lucky ones.

"It's not just a job for them," he said. "It's like they make us all their sons, their brothers. They truly care. I know we're grateful to have them assigned to us. They go the extra mile to make our time here special."

When Salem was chosen to host the national tournament on an annual basis, local officials approached Roger about being a host family. As the president of the local sports foundation for high schools, he thought that was a great idea. So the couple jumped in with both feet in an effort to make the team feel at home.

"My wife and I get into it a little more than the other host families," Roger said. "We meet them at the airport, go to practices, sit behind the bench and cheer them on during the game."

Since the team's magical run to the national title a year ago, the Surbers' interest in the men's basketball team has bordered on obsessive. The couple listens to games on the radio through the Internet, prints season statistics off and have been in touch with UWSP athletics director Frank O'Brien via e-mail.

"We were afraid we were going to jinx them (by) paying so much attention during the season," Bonnie said. "We had a special reason to root for Stevens Point to be here again. We would have been so disappointed had they not won (the sectional)."

UWSP got a chance to repay their hospitality earlier this season. The Surbers were the guest of honor for the regular season game against Whitewater on February 9. They were introduced to the crowd prior to the game and carried the game ball out to center court before the opening tip-off.

O'Brien also took them on a tour of Stevens Point.

"Everyone cheered us and it was so loud," Roger said. "It felt like we were the king and queen of England. Everyone was so nice."

The Surbers admit to being a little superstitious. Everything has been done exactly the same way as a year ago, including traveling the exact same routes to practice. And the couple has been good luck. Teams they've hosted have won the title more often than not.

"It just makes it that much more fun," Roger said.

NCAA DIVISION III
MEN'S FINAL FOUR

Die-hard fans don't miss the bus to see Pointers

Above: The Pointer band, led by Paul Doebler, made the long trip to Salem, VA.

Below: Pointer fans make their presence felt during the Final Four.

TOM CHARLESWORTH

By Scott Williams

SALEM, Va. - Steve Zywicki found getting some sleep difficult. But what is a little sleep deprivation when you have a chance to see the University of Wisconsin-Stevens Point men's basketball team at the Division III Final Four?

"I'm just happy to be here," said Zywicki, assistant director of alumni relations for UWSP. "I'm not a good bus sleeper. There were too many stops, so it took longer than expected."

Zywicki helped organize three busloads of Pointer fans to attend this weekend's tournament at the Salem Civic Center. The interest, or perhaps opportunity, was better this year compared to a year ago when UWSP enjoyed a magical run to the school's first national championship.

Walter Iwanski, a 1962 graduate of the university, is used to long road trips. The Port Edwards resident was on hand to see the Pointers beat Williams (Mass.) 84-82 in the title game last season. Iwanski considers himself a die-hard fan.

"I go up to Point two days a week during the season, usually for a women's game and a men's game," said Iwanski, who moved out of the area for 30 years before returning three years ago. "I went to the women's (championship) game in Terre Haute (Ind.).

"It's nice being a part of something neat. I knew I was going to go right after the sectional. The bus is much easier. I've done enough driving in my life."

Zywicki estimated 150 people took advantage of the buses. He heard of many more who were planning on driving or flying to the tournament.

UWSP assistant athletic director for media relations Jim Strick was informed the school's entire allotment of tickets for the Final Four had been accounted for.

Season ticket holder Sue Hintz missed the event last season.

"I had nothing booked, so I was free to come," Hintz said. "Just the atmosphere of the bus is fun. You might as well get down and dirty. What a cheap ticket for some great entertainment.

"It's so exciting. I have a lot of respect for Jack Bennett and the players. Jason Kalsow is my man. I just cheer him on."

Another aspect of the trip that made it more appealing this season was the departure time. A year ago, the fan busses left early on Thursday morning, forcing people to miss two or three days of school or work. Hintz had to find replacements for her at work for Friday and Monday.

Unlike many of their fellow students, Jeremy Olson and Mike Hanson opted to attend the Final Four rather than spend his spring break in the warmth and sunshine of Florida or Mexico. Olson skipped all of his classes on Friday and missed part of a three-hour lab the previous day. He has no regrets.

"It's definitely going to be worth it," Olson said. "It's fun when everyone making the trip has a common purpose. They're the favorites here and everyone wanted to be here to cheer them on."

TOM CHARLESWORTH

The buses left Stevens Point at approximately 5 p.m. on Thursday and arrived in Salem at 1:30 p.m. eastern standard time on Friday. Despite the absence of sleep and the late arrival, the Pointer fans expected to be in good voice and prepared to cheer UWSP on to what all hope will be back-to-back national championships.

"We barely have enough time to show up at our hotels and get to the Civic Center," Zywicki said. "We've been watching them this long, why not the last two games of the season?"

"There is a lot of excitement to see them repeat. We're confident they're going to play basketball the way they can."

TOM CHARLESWORTH

TOM CHARLESWORTH

Top Left and Right: *Pointer fashion statements were seen all over the Salem Civic Center.*

Bottom Left: *Nearly 150 fans of the University of Wisconsin-Stevens Point men's basketball team board buses to travel to Salem, VA., to cheer on the Pointers as they defend their NCAA Division III National Championship in the Final Four.*

DOUG WOJCIK

NCAA DIVISION III
MEN'S FINAL FOUR

ONE MORE TO GO

UWSP advances to title game after semifinal victory over York; will take on Rochester

By Scott Williams

Above: Steve Hicklin steals the ball and goes in for a layup during the first half.

Below: Jason Kalsow pulls up for a three-pointer.

TOM CHARLESWORTH

TOM CHARLESWORTH

SALEM, Va. - Seeing its dream for back-to-back Division III national championships end in the semifinals wasn't an option for the University of Wisconsin-Stevens Point men's basketball team.

Looking every bit the part of the defending national champions, UWSP made itself comfortable in a building that is home to many fond memories. The top-ranked Pointers came out on a mission in the first half and easily deposed of York (Pa.) College 81-58 in the semifinal matchup at the Salem Civic Center on Friday.

All that stands in the Pointers' (28-3) way of a date with history is Rochester (N.Y.) University (25-4). Tipoff is set for 4 p.m. At stake is a chance to become the first team to repeat as national champion since UW-Platteville in 1998-99.

"We're playing a whale of a basketball team tomorrow," UWSP coach Jack Bennett said. "It's going to be another terrific championship game similar to last year. At the worst we'll be national runners-up, and with the national title last year."

York (28-3) can thank Trinity College for awakening a giant in the sectional final. Pointer senior forward Jason Kalsow came out like a man possessed against the Spartans. After seeing his 63-game streak of scoring in double figures end, Kalsow nearly put up a triple double in the next to last game of his Pointer career. He finished with 20 points, 12 rebounds and eight assists.

"I struggled a little in the sectional," said Kalsow, who didn't stop there. He also blocked five shots and didn't commit a turnover in 39 nearly flawless minutes. "It was not a goal I had to come out and put up numbers like that."

York coach Jeff Gamber was at a loss at how to defense the Pointers.

"That is a tremendous stat line. I would vote him (Kalsow) for MVP," Gamber said of Kalsow. "You can't take everything away. They have a lot of weapons and there is a reason why they're the defending national champions and a reason they're the No. 1 team in the country."

Included in the Pointers' arsenal are Kyle Grusczynski and Eric Maus, who combined for 25 points. Grusczynski, in particular, supplied the Pointers with a much-needed boost off the bench in the first half. He had eight of his points in the opening 20 minutes, including a pair of 3-pointers.

"Kyle has definitely been playing his best ball at the end of the year," Maus said. "He's been coming into his own. Kyle has all the potential in the world and we're seeing it now."

His ability to hit from long distance would be an omen of things to come. An 8-for-15 performance from behind the arc in the first half enabled UWSP to build as much as a 19-point lead. The Pointers' advantage stood 40-26 at intermission.

"You have to give Stevens Point a lot of credit," Gamber said. "They played great right from the start and shot the 3-pointer extremely well. They're a really good team that played well."

Gamber, who saw his team's 14-game winning streak snapped, figured stopping the Pointers would be nearly impossible. So his hope was that the Spartans could outscore them, not exactly a great formula for success against a team that ranks second in the nation, allowing only 56.2 points a game.

The Pointers spent most of the night switching from a 3-2 and 1-3-1 zone to man-to-man and York was never able to find a comfort zone.

"Defensively, we changed up enough to maybe put them on their heels a little bit," Bennett said. "Our priority was to make everything tough for them. The biggest thing was to minimize their rebounding. We said that was the one thing we had to do or we were in trouble."

York came into the game out rebounding opponents by nine boards a game. The final rebounding numbers Friday: Stevens Point 39, York 27.

Below Left: Nick Bennett with a jumper for two.

Below Center: Eric Maus shoots the wide open jumper.

Below Right: The NCAA Mascot gets the crowd pumped up.

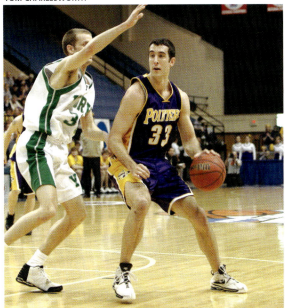

Above: Nick Bennett looks for a crease in the York defense.

POINTERS 81, SPARTANS 58

UW-Stevens Point (81): Steve Hicklin 2-5 1-2 6, Nick Bennett 6-15 0-0 16, Jon Krull 3-5 2-2 9, Jason Kalsow 7-16 3-4 20, Eric Maus 5-11 2-2 12, Kyle Grusczynski 5-9 1-1 13, Matt Bouche 1-1 0-0 2, Brian Bauer 1-3 0-0 3. Totals 30-65 9-11 81.

York College (58): Brad Zerfing 2-5 2-3 6, Kenny Fass 5-10 0-0 13, Brandon Bushey 4-10 2-2 11, Ben Seibert 2-3 0-0 4, Brian Singer 5-12 0-1 10, Chad McGowan 3-5 3-4 9, Paddy Lee 1-3 0-0 3, Josh Wurtz 1-2 0-0 2, Chris Folland 0-1 0-0 0, Pat D'Arcy 0-1 0-0 0. Totals 23-52 7-10 58.

UW-Stevens Point	40	41	-81
York College	26	32	-58

3-point goals: Stevens Point 12-24 (Hicklin 1-3, Bennett 4-7, Krull 1-1, Kalsow 3-5, Grusczynski 2-5, Bauer 1-3), York 5-15 (Zerfing 0-2, Fass 3-4, Bushey 1-5, McGowan 0-1, Lee 1-1, Wurtz 0-1, D'Arcy 0-1). Total fouls: Stevens Point 11, York 14. Fouled out: None. Rebounds: Stevens Point 39 (Kalsow, Maus 12), York 27 (Seibert 5). Turnovers: Stevens Point 6, York 11.

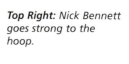

TOM CHARLESWORTH

Top Right: Nick Bennett goes strong to the hoop.

Bottom Left to Right:

• Coach Bennett scouts the Rochester semifinal game.

• Shawn Lee calls out the offense.

• Pointers 81, York 58

• A Pointer cheerleader cheers her team into the National Championship game.

TOM CHARLESWORTH

Above Left: Jason Kalsow looks to pass the ball into a posting Nick Bennett. Kalsow and Bennett combined for 36 points against York.

TOM CHARLESWORTH

TOM CHARLESWORTH

TOM CHARLESWORTH

TOM CHARLESWORTH

Below: The color guard walks to mid-court for the national anthem.

TOM CHARLESWORTH

NCAA DIVISION III
MEN'S FINAL FOUR
NATIONAL CHAMPS
UWSP men's basketball coasts to championship repeat

By Scott Williams

SALEM, Va. - All season the University of Wisconsin-Stevens Point men's basketball team had been about the sum being greater than the parts.

That unselfish attitude made the Pointers a "team" in the truest sense of the word.

Make that the best team in Division III for the second year running.

The Pointers put an exclamation point on a remarkable two-year run by becoming only the third men's team to win consecutive national titles with a 73-49 demolition of Rochester (N.Y.) University at the Salem Civic Center on Saturday night.

"I think this one is a little bit more satisfying," said senior guard Nick Bennett, one of three Pointers named to the all-tournament team. "It's definitely a different feeling. Last year we sneaked up on people. This time everyone was geared up for us and wanted to give us their best shot.

"I guess it goes to show what a bunch of skinny white guys from Wisconsin, and one from Illinois, can do when they put their minds to it."

The win puts UWSP in the elite company of North Park (Ill.) and UW-Platteville as teams to win back-to-back titles, and the first since 1998-99 (Platteville).

Bennett, who failed to score in the opening half, played out of his mind over the final 20 minutes. He scored 18 points in the second half as the Pointers (29-3) turned a potential nail-biter into the largest margin of victory in championship game history. But the Stevens Point native was only a small part of a complete team effort.

Sophomore Jon Krull came up huge, especially in the first half when he scored 13 of his team-high 22 points. Eric Maus, a senior, made his presence felt on the defensive end where he held Rochester standout Seth Hauben to eight points - 11 points below his season average.

"When a team dedicates itself to making plays for one another, it shows there are basketball teams still out there who play the game the way it's supposed to be played," said UWSP coach Jack Bennett, who won his 200th career game as the Pointers' coach.

"There were high expectations on this team

most of the season, and for them to accomplish something like this goes beyond good to terrifically special."

Clinging to a 28-25 lead at intermission, UWSP continued a season-long trend of playing lights out in the second half.

"Part of it is we've been in so many big games that no one gets rattled," said Jason Kalsow, who was named the Most Valuable Player of the Final Four.

The Pointers just might have played their best half of basketball in their biggest game.

"When we start clicking on all cylinders, we're a handful to defend," coach Bennett said.

UWSP was a couple handfuls worth in the final 20 minutes. But to shoot 64 percent, including a red-hot 6-for-11 effort from behind the arc, in the most important half of the season is mind-boggling.

What had the makings of a pressure-packed finish suddenly turned into a lopsided affair. A 27-10 run to open the second half sealed the Yellowjackets' fate and season.

"Once they got separation and got a 12-point lead, they had the discipline, experience and talent to take time off with each possession," Rochester coach Mike Neer said. "We needed to stay close and then the pressure falls back on them as the favorites."

With Bennett in foul trouble, the responsibility of keeping the Pointers close in the first half fell on the broad shoulders of Krull, who took full advantage of physical mismatches inside against the smaller Yellowjacket guards. Once the rest of the team caught up with the Marshall native, the Yellowjackets never stood a chance.

"It just kind of shook out that way," said Krull of his starring role. "When you have five guys that can score, teams might stop two of

TOM CHARLESWORTH

Top: Voice of the Pointers' Scott Krueger and color man John Zellmer call the national championship game for WSPT.

Right: Head Coach Jack Bennett walks to the court for the national championship game.

TOM CHARLESWORTH

them, but then the other three are going to beat you."

In a fitting conclusion to an unprecedented career, Kalsow sent down a slam for his final basket as a Pointer.

Coach Bennett was filled with mixed emotions. Ecstatic over the feat of winning back-to-back national championships, he was torn by the realization he'll never get to coach this special group of seniors, including his son, again.

"I've said it before, but I wish I could freeze these guys and this moment in time," coach Bennett said.

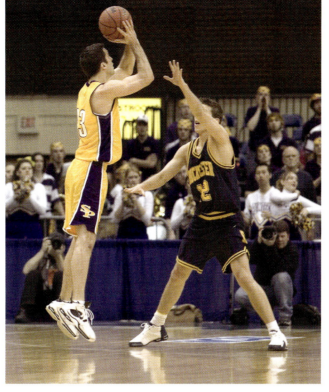

RYAN COLEMAN

POINTERS 73, ROCHESTER 49

Rochester (25-5) - Hauben, Seth 2-5 4-4 8, Onyiriuka, Jon 4-8 6-10 14, McAllister, Brendan 2-7 0-0 6, Juron, Jeff 1-7 2-2 5, Perez, Gabe 1-4 0-0 2, Mee, Ryan 1-3 0-0 3, Canty, Joe 0-1 0-0 0, Thorne, Will 0-0 0-0 0, Brackney, Tim 4-11 0-0 11, Milbrand, Dan 0-0 0-0 0, Ndubizu, Uche 0-0 0-0 0, Snider, Eric 0-0 0-0 0

UW-Stevens Point (29-3) - Krull, Jon 8-12 6-6 22, Kalsow, Jason 6-13 1-1 15, Maus, Eric 2-3 0-0 4, Hicklin, Steve 2-2 2-2 7, Bennett, Nick 6-9 2-3 18 Lee, Shawn 0-0 0-0 0, Hirsch, Brett 0-0 0-0 0, Kalsow, Brad 0-1 0-0 0, Gruszczynski, Kyle 1-5 0-0 2, Krautkramer, Cory 0-0 0-0 0, Bouche, Matt 0-0 0-0 0, Bauer, Brian 1-2 0-0 3, Prey, Mike 0-0 0-0 0, Awe, Gbenga 1-1 0-0 2, Doyle, Tyler 0-0 0-0 0

Rochester	25	24	- 49
UW-Stevens Point	28	45	- 73

3-point goals: Stevens Point 12-24 (Hicklin 1-3, Bennett 4-7, Krull 1-1, Kalsow 3-5, Gruszczynski 2-5, Bauer 1-3), Rochester 5-15 (Zerfing 0-2, Fass 3-4, Bushey 1-5, McGowan 0-1, Lee 1-1, Wurtz 0-1, D'Arcy 0-1). Total fouls: Stevens Point 13, Rochester 16. Fouled out: None. Rebounds: Stevens Point 26 (Krull 7), Rochester 29 (Onyiriuka 11). Turnovers: Stevens Point 5, Rochester 10. Attendance: 2877

RYAN COLEMAN

Counter Clockwise from Top:
• *Nick Bennett for three.*
• *Rochester guard Tim Brackney kept the Yellowjackets close with his first half shooting.*
• *Coach Bennett looks on as Pointer All-American Jason Kalsow knocks down a three-pointer.*

RYAN COLEMAN

Left: Jason Kalsow and Nick Bennett take the court for the national championship game.

Right: The opening tip in the 2004-2005 NCAA Division III National Championship game.

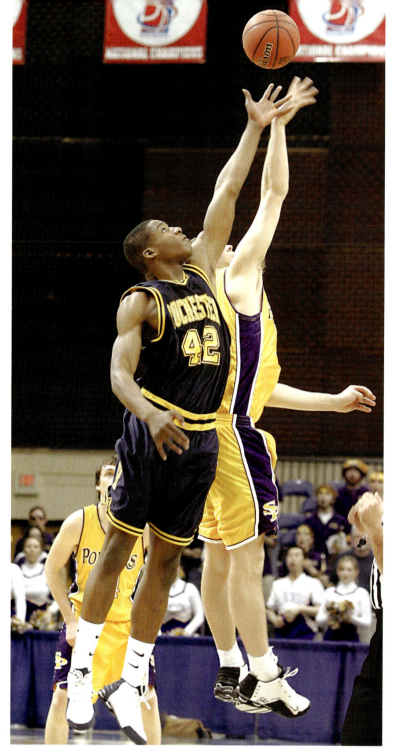

Top Left: *Head Coach Jack Bennett and son Nick share a moment after capturing their second national championship.*

Bottom Left: *Jason Kalsow and Eric Maus defend Rochester All-American Seth Hauben during first half action.*

Right: *All-American Jason Kalsow goes up for his final two points as a Pointer: a slam dunk.*

TOM CHARLESWORTH

TOM CHARLESWORTH

TOM CHARLESWORTH

Left: Eric Maus works for rebounding position as Kyle Grusczynski shoots a jump shot.

Right Top: A UWSP fan cheers for the Pointers.

Right Bottom: A Jon Krull fan and the soon to be Mrs. Kyle Grusczynski.

TOM CHARLESWORTH

Left: These Pointer fans sum up their experience in Salem.

Right: Chancellor Linda Bunnell shows her support for the Pointers.

TOM CHARLESWORTH

Left: Eric Maus goes up for two.

Right: After being held scoreless in the first half, All-American Nick Bennett scorched Rochester for 18 second half points.

TOM CHARLESWORTH

RYAN COLEMAN

Above: National Coach of the Year Jack Bennett works the officials during the national championship game.

Right: Point guard Steve Hicklin makes his free throw.

TOM CHARLESWORTH

Above: The 2004-05 NCAA Division III National Champions.

NCAA DIVISION III
NATIONAL CHAMPIONSHIP GAME

Clockwise starting with Top Left:
- *Long-time Pointer supporters Jim and Nancy Lamar and Jerry Wilson and Sandy Konop.*
- *The Pointers bench erupts after winning their second consecutive national championship.*
- *Head Coach Jack Bennett and senior All-Americans Jason Kalsow and Nick Bennett are interviewed by Eddie Fogler after the national championship game.*
- *Provost and Vice Chancellor for Academic Affairs, Virginia Helm, and Assistant Chancellor for Student Affairs, Bob Tomlinson, cheer on the Pointers in Salm.*

KRULL COMES UP BIG
TO LEAD POINTERS

Below: Jon Krull led the Pointers with 22 points in the national championship victory over Rochester.

By Scott Williams

TOM CHARLESWORTH

SALEM, Va. - When coaches mention the University of Wisconsin-Stevens Point men's basketball team, Jason Kalsow and Nick Bennett are the first names to come to mind.

Rochester (N.Y.) University coach Mike Neer is going to have nightmares about the Pointers' Jon Krull. Krull stepped onto the biggest stage of all and grabbed the spotlight with a game-high 22 points to help the Pointers smash the Yellowjackets 73-49 in the NCAA Division III championship game at the Salem Civic Center on Saturday night.

In the process, UWSP became just the third team to win back-to-back national titles.

"They kept getting the ball inside to Krull," Neer said. "He scored more than 2,000 points in high school as a bruiser inside and he's being guarded by a point guard."

That all but sums up the dilemma most teams face against the Pointers. When too much attention is paid to the likes of Bennett and Kalsow, there are still three or four more weapons to be concerned about. On this night, Krull found himself matched up with much smaller guards most of the game and, at 6-foot-4, 230 pounds, he could bully his way around the basket.

"When you have five players who can score, it makes it tough to defend us," Krull said. "If you concentrate on two of us, then the other three are going to beat you."

Krull inflicted a major beating on the Yellowjackets in the first half. He scored 13 of his 22 points in the opening 20 minutes as Kalsow and Bennett received most of the attention. Krull kept the Pointers close until the so-called "stars" of the team could get going.

"We've got great role players, and Jon Krull was big tonight," UWSP coach Jack Bennett said. "Other players can pick it up when necessary, and Jon got the lid off the basket for us tonight."

Rochester tried just about everyone on its bench to contain or slow down Krull to no avail. No matter who the Yellowjackets threw at him, Krull simply overpowered him.

"There is so much talk about Kalsow and Bennett, then they come at you with their third and fourth options and they can hurt you," Neer said.

Krull has a history of playing well in the Final Four. As a freshman a year ago, Krull scored 25 points in a semifinal win over John Carroll (Ohio) University. Krull's performance this time around earned him a spot on the all-tournament team alongside Kalsow, the MVP, and Bennett.

"Our motion offense is not predicated on special plays for one person," Krull said. "We just take what the defense gives you. If it's there, it's there. Tonight it was for me."

UWSP FANS
WELCOME CHAMPS HOME

By Kelly McBride

Above: Coach Bennett signs autographs for two young Pointer fans.

Below: The five seniors share a laugh during the welcome home ceremony. From left, Jason Kalsow, Nick Bennett, Eric Maus, Tamaris Relerford and Kyle Grusczynski.

With the winningest coach in school history, two first-team all-Americans, the Division III player of the year and back-to-back national championships, the University of Wisconsin-Stevens Point men's basketball team has plenty to celebrate.

And celebrate they did at a Wednesday rally belatedly welcoming home the champs following their second consecutive national victory March 19.

Facing bleachers jam-packed with eager students and community members sitting shoulder-to-shoulder, the players and coaches doled out as much praise as they received, thanking everyone who made their repeat trip to Salem, Va., a reality. From the pep band members to cheerleaders and scores of fans who made the trip to Salem, the Pointers made sure no one was forgotten.

"I was a band member," senior guard Tamaris Relerford told a cheering pep band. "First chair."

Although Wednesday's rally was a long time in coming, it was worth it for the fans and players, many said. A rally originally scheduled for March 20 was put on hold because of a flight cancellation. But because many players went on spring break following their championship run, the delay meant every Pointer was there to celebrate.

"It's just a culmination to a great career," senior guard Kyle Grusczynski said. "It's huge. ... Last year, we didn't have a celebration like this. It's just incredible."

Wednesday's rally also brought back championship memories for some fans who made the trip to Salem to cheer on the purple and gold. Sophomore women's basketball player Becky Pepper said the experience was unparalleled - especially because she got to watch her boyfriend, Pointer All-American Nick Bennett.

"It was awesome," she said. "Watching all the confetti fall. ... I know how hard (Bennett) worked, how determined and dedicated he was. ... It was just awesome to be there."

Although members of the Stevens Point community, young and old, were well-represented at Wednesday's event, some fans came from a bit further away to welcome home the team. Seventeen-year-old Allison Jackan of Marshfield made the trek to cheer for the Pointers. Being a part of it all was a highlight of the evening, Jackan said.

"Just the whole excitement of it," she said. "All the fans. They're so proud of everybody."

In addition to the students, faculty, administration and community members, some local politicians came to extend their congratulations.

Rep. Louis Molepske Jr., D-Stevens Point - sporting a bright purple tie - presented the team with a plaque on behalf of the Wisconsin State Legislature.

Mayor Gary Wescott also was on hand. He had one word for the crowd at Quandt Fieldhouse, he said. "And I believe I can accurately reflect the mood of this crowd," he said to cheers, "when I say 'Three-peat.' "

UWSP Chancellor Linda Bunnell also addressed the crowd, reading a proclamation from Gov. Jim Doyle that declared Wednesday UW-Stevens Point Pointers Day. A portion of the governor's proclamation lauded the fact that 16 of the 19 Pointers hail from Wisconsin. But Bunnell also had a message for the three Illinois natives, Jason and Brad

Kalsow and John Gleich.

"Jason, Brad, John," Bunnell said with a smile, "I hereby declare you Wisconsin natives."

Then, to laughter and applause from the crowd, Bunnell quipped, "I wish I could refund your out-of-state tuition."

Still, the biggest cheers were reserved for brief speeches from the Pointer seniors and a heartfelt address from Pointer Coach Jack Bennett. At the end, Bennett led the crowd to their feet for a cheer shared by Pointers and community members alike.

"We only do this for certain big moments," he said. "The three cheers for the good guys."

DOUG WOJCIK

DOUG WOJCIK

DOUG WOJCIK

Top Left: *UWSP Chancellor Linda Bunnell presents Head Coach Jack Bennett with a proclamation from Governor Jim Doyle that declared Wednesday March 30, 2005 as UW-Stevens Point Pointers Day.*

Top Right: *Coach Bennett addresses the crowd.*

Bottom Left: *Coach Bennett receives a standing ovation from his team.*

AWARDS

Jason Kalsow named Division III Player of the Year

Nick Bennett earns All-American

Jack Bennett National Coach of the Year

By Kelly McBride

After winning a second straight NCAA Division III men's basketball championship and rewriting UW-Stevens Point's career records book, senior Jason Kalsow has been named the Division III Player of the Year by the National Association of Basketball Coaches. Kalsow was also the Basketball Times National Player of the Year and a first-team All-American selection by D3hoops.com. Teammate Nick Bennett was also named first-team All-American by Basketball Times and D3hoops.com, while earning third-team NABC All-American honors. Coach Jack Bennett was selected as the Basketball Times Coach of the Year.

Kalsow's Player of the Year honor marks the second straight year a Wisconsin Intercollegiate Athletic Conference player has won the award after Rich Melzer of UW-River Falls was selected last year. UW-Platteville's Merrill Brunson is the league's only other winner in its 23-year history, claiming the honor in 1999. Kalsow will be honored at the NCAA Division I Final Four in St. Louis at the NABC awards banquet on April 3.

His award comes just two days after UW-Stevens Point's Amanda Nechuta was announced as the Division III Women's Player of the Year. It marks the first time in any NCAA division that a school has had both Player of the Year winners in the same year. In fact, UW-Stevens Point becomes the first Division III school ever to have both a men's and women's national Player of the Year in its history.

Kalsow, a 6-7 forward from Huntley, Ill., was the Most Valuable Player of this year's Division III final four and started all 121 games in his four-year career. He is UW-Stevens Point's all-time leading scorer and rebounder with 1,859 points and 883 rebounds. He also had a school record 731 field goals made and was second in school history with 465 assists.

Kalsow is the third NABC first-team All-American in school history, joining Terry Porter in 1985 and Brant Bailey in 2000. He led the WIAC with 19.1 points per game, 4.4 assists per game and a 48.9 three-point field goal percentage. He was also second in the league in rebounding at 7.4 per game. He ranked among the top 15 in all 12 WIAC statistical categories.

Nick Bennett, a 6-5 guard who played at Stevens Point Area Senior High, finished third in school history in career scoring with 1,646 points. He set a school record and ranks second in WIAC history with 232 career three-pointers and eclipsed his own single-season school record with 88 three-pointers this year. Bennett ranked second in the WIAC in scoring at 18.3 points per game and was sixth in the nation in free throw shooting at 89.4 percent. Bennett was at his best in the NCAA tournament, averaging 23.2 points and shooting 57.0 percent from three-point range in 12 career tournament games.

Jack Bennett was the D-III News National Coach of the Year last season and is the third coach to guide a team to back-to-back national titles. He is UW-Stevens Point's all-time winningest coach and ranks second among active Division III coaches in winning percentage with a 200-56 career record.

TOM CHARLESWORTH

Left: First-team All-American and Division III National Player of the Year Jason Kalsow.

UWSP: THE EPITOME
OF A COMPLETE TEAM

UWSP SPORTS INFORMATION OFFICE

2004-2005 National Champions

By Scott Williams

There is no denying who the so-called "stars" of the University of Wisconsin-Stevens Point men's basketball team were over the past couple seasons.

Without Jason Kalsow, a do-everything 6-foot-7 forward, and sharp-shooting Nick Bennett there almost certainly are no back-to-back NCAA Division III national championships.

Heck. Bennett and Kalsow, respectively, were named the most outstanding player at the Final Four the last two seasons.

The dynamic scoring tandem made life miserable for opposing teams. There were times when teams could silence either Bennett or Kalsow, but never both.

Their legacy will be forever remembered in the Pointer record books. Kalsow concluded his career as the school's all-time leading scorer (1,859) and rebounder.

Bennett, who finished third on the all-time scoring list with 1,646 - three points behind No. 2 Tim Naegeli - and made more 3-pointers than any other player in school history, is the epitome of a self-made player.

His basketball options coming out of Stevens Point Area Senior High were slim and none. The son of Pointer coach Jack Bennett, Nick turned himself into a first team All-American through determination and hard work.

Every basketball team needs a star or two. At crunch time a team needs someone it can call upon as a go-to player to come through in the clutch.

But there are no national titles, in all likelihood, without Kyle Grusczynski, Eric Maus, Jon Krull, Tamaris Relerford, and more recently, Steve Hicklin.

No one other than Kalsow and Nick Bennett have admitted as much. Their jobs would have been a whole lot tougher without a Grusczynski as the quintessential sixth-man.

The Seymour native played any of five positions on the court and contributed in one form or another. Grusczynski might drain a 3-pointer, deflect a pass as the point man in the 3-2 zone or hand out a key assist.

SEASON STATS
UW-Stevens Point Men's Basketball — All Games

```
RECORD:             OVERALL    HOME      AWAY      NEUTRAL
ALL GAMES..........  (29-3)    (18-0)    (8-3)     (3-0)
CONFERENCE.........  (13-3)    (8-0)     (5-3)     (0-0)
NON-CONFERENCE.....  (16-0)    (10-0)    (3-0)     (3-0)
```

			---TOTAL---			---3-PTS---			----REBOUNDS----												
## Player	GP-GS	Min	Avg	FG-FGA	Pct	3FG-FGA	Pct	FT-FTA	Pct	Off	Def	Tot	Avg	PF	FO	A	TO	Blk	Stl	Pts	Avg
44 Kalsow, Jason......	32-32	1038	32.4	227-406	.559	43-89	.483	114-146	.781	68	170	238	7.4	77	1	142	64	41	36	611	19.1
33 Bennett, Nick......	32-32	1027	32.1	194-388	.500	88-194	.454	110-123	.894	18	90	108	3.4	60	0	81	57	4	19	586	18.3
34 Krull, Jon.........	32-32	754	23.6	102-184	.554	8-25	.320	62-80	.775	37	85	122	3.8	37	0	50	31	6	45	274	8.6
50 Maus, Eric.........	30-28	808	26.9	86-149	.577	1-1	1.000	45-56	.804	47	105	152	5.1	56	1	61	24	12	20	218	7.3
10 Relerford, Tamaris.	28-27	681	24.3	41-101	.406	34-80	.425	26-34	.765	9	35	44	1.6	40	0	49	31	1	22	142	5.1
25 Grusczynski, Kyle..	32-3	578	18.1	49-118	.415	25-75	.333	18-26	.692	18	59	77	2.4	44	0	44	21	14	19	141	4.4
24 Hicklin, Steve.....	26-4	268	10.3	24-48	.500	6-25	.240	22-28	.786	3	15	18	0.7	19	0	20	12	1	7	76	2.9
55 Gleich, John.......	2-0	4	2.0	2-2	1.000	0-0	.000	1-1	1.000	1	1	2	1.0	0	0	0	0	0	0	5	2.5
22 Kalsow, Brad.......	28-0	238	8.5	20-46	.435	9-26	.346	12-15	.800	11	25	36	1.3	22	0	11	9	3	3	61	2.2
42 Bauer, Brian.......	31-1	292	9.4	26-56	.464	10-22	.455	2-5	.400	14	23	37	1.2	42	0	13	14	4	12	64	2.1
20 Hirsch, Brett......	22-0	99	4.5	17-31	.548	0-1	.000	8-20	.400	5	16	21	1.0	13	0	5	4	0	6	42	1.9
12 Lee, Shawn.........	24-0	208	8.7	11-19	.579	8-13	.615	10-10	1.000	1	8	9	0.4	16	0	14	13	0	6	40	1.7
52 Awe, Gbenga.......	27-0	159	5.9	13-37	.351	0-0	.000	10-21	.476	12	34	46	1.7	30	0	8	19	4	9	36	1.3
45 Prey, Mike.........	27-1	137	5.1	7-18	.389	0-0	.000	6-13	.462	8	22	30	1.1	11	0	3	13	3	3	20	0.7
40 Bouche, Matt......	20-0	57	2.9	5-13	.385	0-0	.000	4-5	.800	5	5	10	0.5	6	0	0	2	1	3	14	0.7
32 Krautkramer, Cory.	21-0	64	3.0	3-19	.158	0-2	.000	5-8	.625	2	7	9	0.4	10	0	2	4	0	2	11	0.5
98 Doyle, Tyler......	4-0	12	3.0	0-0	.000	0-0	.000	2-4	.500	0	0	0	0.0	1	0	0	2	0	0	2	0.5
50 Leahy, Zach.......	1-0	1	1.0	0-0	.000	0-0	.000	0-0	.000	0	0	0	0.0	0	0	0	0	0	0	0	0.0
TEAM................										32	57	89	2.9			0	2				
Total...............	32	6425		827-1635	.506	232-553	.420	457-595	.768	291	757	1048	32.8	484	3	503	322	94	212	2343	73.2
Opponents..........	32	6425		607-1620	.375	184-630	.292	396-544	.728	320	596	916	28.6	562	-	316	387	60	130	1794	56.1

```
SCORE BY PERIODS:           1st    2nd   OT    Total
---------------------------  ----  ----  ----  ----
UW-Stevens Point...........  1083  1252    8  - 2343
Opponents..................   800   987    7  - 1794

DEADBALL REBOUNDS:          OFF   DEF  TOTAL
---------------------------  ---  -----  -----
UW-Stevens Point...........   56    16    72
Opponents..................   68     3    71
```

ODE TO THE POINTERS

By Tim "Shoe" Sullivan

Point won it all
in the year '04.
So then they thought:
let's win one more.

Coach Bennett was dining
with his spoon and fork.
He'd soon be playing
the men from York.

Out came the napkin,
Coach let out a groan.
"They like man-to-man,
so we'll go with the zone."

The defense was great,
and the Pointers were racin'.
The game came down
to the forward named Jason.

Kalsow went inside and out,
and shot the ball plenty.
A look at the stats,
and you see he got 20.

The coach was happy,
you could tell by the smile.
He also got 25
from Maus and Kyle.

So York went down -
81-58.
One win to go
in a season so great.

Rochester came next,
the crown on the line.
If the Pointers could win,
well, everything's fine.

With Tamaris still out,
Hicklin went on the point.
The Salem gym
was one noisy joint.

Krull started out fast,
no need to worry.
The Pointers' offense
was in no hurry.

But then came the bombs
from Jason and Bauer.
Coach B. had no reason
to stand up and holler.

Maus came up big,
and Nick hit his 3's.
The Pointer shots
were falling with ease.

The Pointers kept shooting,
the net in their sights.
As they kept drilling,
it was turn out the lights.

The Kalsows and Bennett,
with Kyle and Maus.
Sure was some skill
in Virginia's Big House.

Add Krull and Lee,
with Prey and Bauer.
How could this not
be Point's finest hour?

73-49
was the final score.
And the men from Point:
National Champs once more.

team

We're proud to cover a team that embodies everything that College sport aspires to become.

Congratulations UWSP Pointers on your oustanding achievements.

Bryon Graff

Gary Brilowski

Jessob Reisbeck

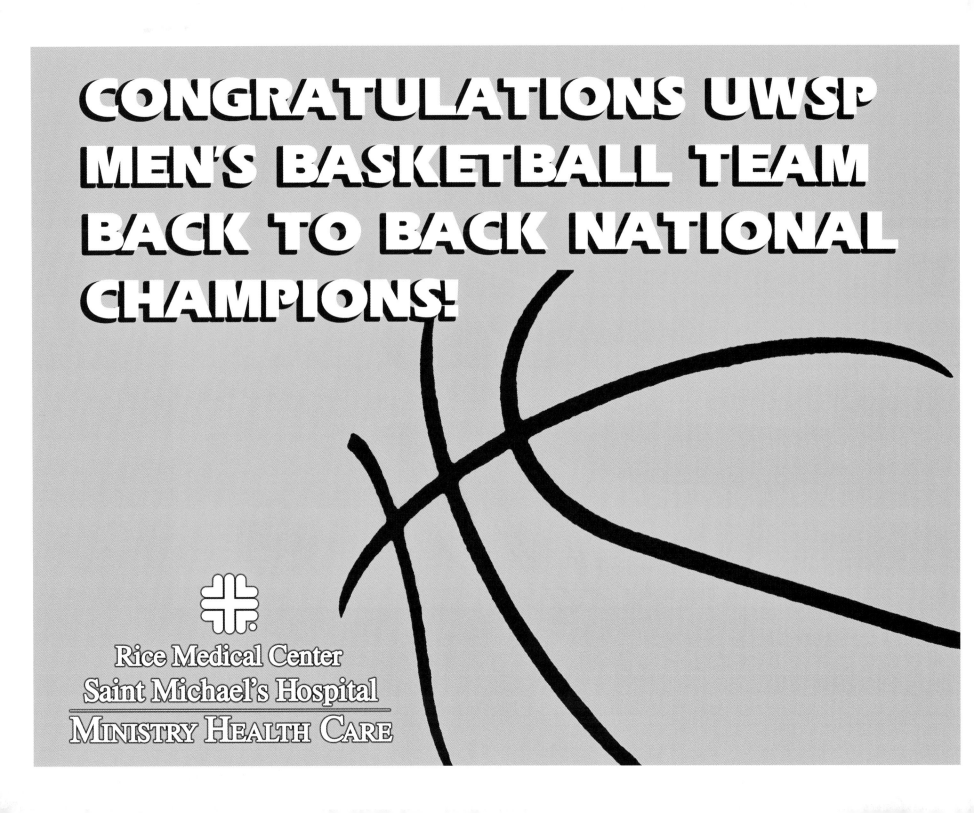

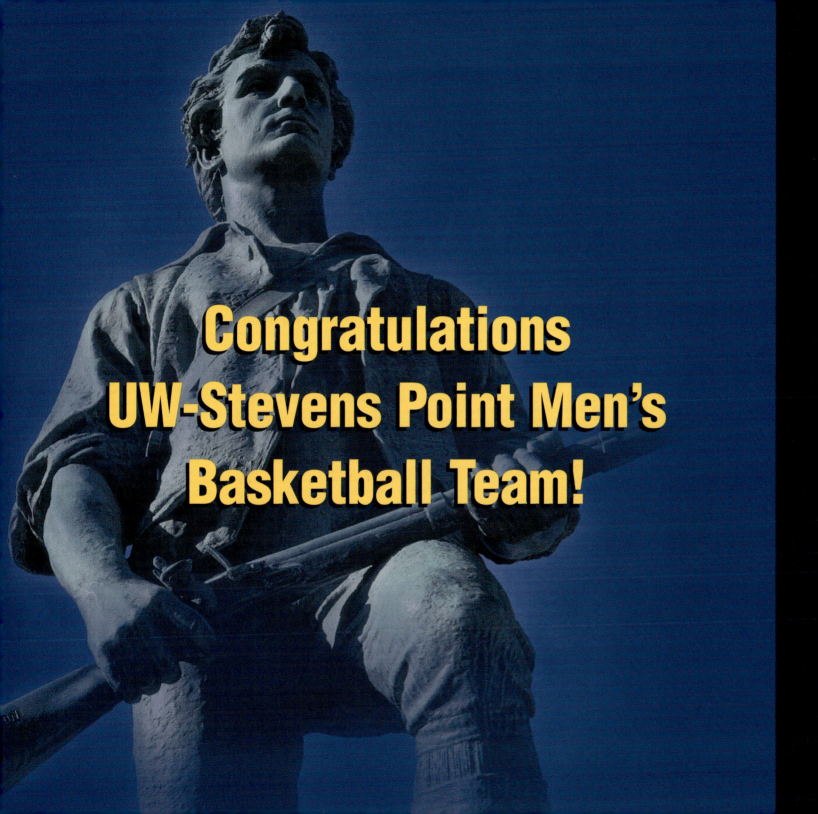

Congratulations to thePointers 2004-2005 National Champs

301 N. GREEN AVE • STEVENS POINT, WI 54481 • 715-341-2440

Congratulations

2004, 2005 NATIONAL CHAMPIONS

THANKS FOR DRIVING HOME ANOTHER CHAMPIONSHIP!

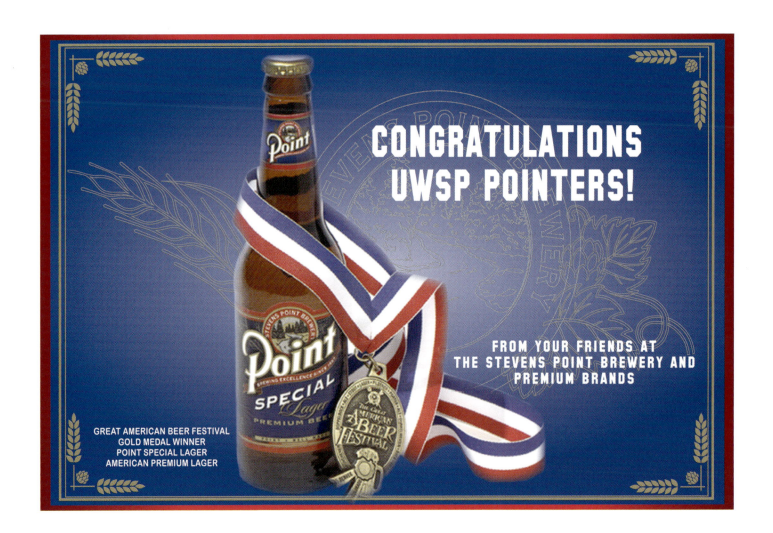